D1087876

Passage East

The saloon of an Irrawaddy steamer, 1903.

PASSAGE EAST

Illustrated and Written by Ian Marshall

Commentary by John Maxtone-Graham

Howell Press

Paintings and text copyright © 1997 by Ian Marshall
Commentary copyright © 1997 by John Maxtone-Graham

All rights reserved.

This book, or any portions thereof, may not be reproduced or transmitted in any form or by any means, electronic or mechanical, including photocopying, recording, or by any information storage and retrieval system, without permission in writing from the publisher, except for brief quotations in critical reviews or articles.

Designed by Carolyn Weary Brandt
Edited by Jamie L. Bronner and Kristina Redmond

Library of Congress Cataloging-in-Publication Data
(Provided by Quality Books, Inc.)

Marshall, Ian (Ian H.)
    Passage east / illustrated and written by Ian Marshall ;
commentary by John Maxtone-Graham. -- 1st ed.
    p. cm.
    Includes bibliographical references and index.
    ISBN: 1-57427-069-9

    1. Steamboats--History--19th century--Pictorial works. 2.
Merchant ships--History--19th century--Pictorial works. 3. Ocean
travel--History--Pictorial works. 4. Peninsular and Oriental Steam
Navigation Company--Pictorial works.   I. Maxtone-Graham, John.
II. Title.

VM615.M37 1997   623.8'24
                                     QBI97-41218

Printed in Hong Kong

Published by Howell Press, Inc.,
1147 River Road, Suite 2,
Charlottesville, Virginia 22901.
Telephone: (804) 977-4006

First Printing

This book is dedicated to

Her Majesty Queen Elizabeth the Queen Mother

Lady of the Garter, Lady of the Thistle, CI, GMVO,
OBE, Dame Grand Cross of the Order of St. John,
Royal Victorian Chain, Lord Warden and Admiral
of the Cinque Ports and Constable of Dover Castle

who was there.

A splendid bronze sphinx, one of a pair which watch over Cleopatra's Needle on the Thames Embankment in London.

For many people, the journey to the East started nearby, on a train leaving from Charing Cross Station. The 3500-year-old obelisk known as Cleopatra's Needle was presented to Britain by Mohammed Ali, Khedive of Egypt, in 1819. It was given in commemoration of Nelson's great victory over the French fleet at the Battle of the Nile in 1798 and the defeat of the army of occupation by Abercromby at Alexandria in 1801. His gift was left lying in the sand until 1878, when the 70-foot granite monolith was placed in an iron tube, towed to England by sea, and erected on its present site.

Obelisks, unlike sphinges, were always made in pairs, and the counterpart of Cleopatra's Needle was given to the United States of America and erected in Central Park, New York, in 1880.

CONTENTS

Watercolor Paintings by Ian Marshall

Watercolor Sketches

Photographs

Maps

ACKNOWLEDGMENTS

I want to thank and record my indebtedness to my dear wife Jean, once again, for her endless patience, encouragement, and word-processing; to Stephen Rabson, Group Information Manager of P & O S.N. Co., for generously devoting his time, and his special knowledge, to enlightening a neophyte; to David Hodge of the National Maritime Museum archives at the Brassfoundry in Woolwich, for help beyond the call of duty; to Louie Howland, John Elliot, Kate Van Liere, and Kinnear Macdonald for friendly advice and editorial help; to Oliver Swann for continuing support and never-failing enthusiasm; and to my colleague John Maxtone-Graham and publisher Ross Howell for making the idea of *Passage East* into a reality.

Singapore waterfront, c. 1900.

A number of countries and places mentioned in the text now have different names. I have used the names and the spelling which would have been familiar to nineteenth century passengers.

Passage East

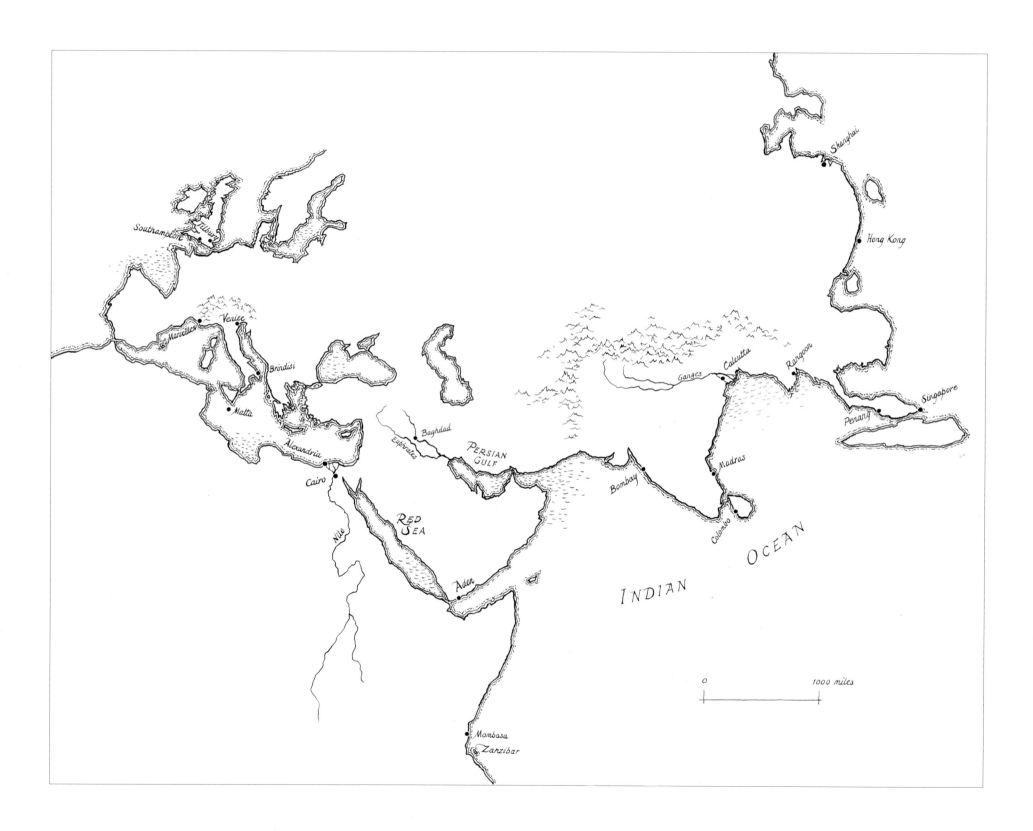

Passage East

Just when the eyes of the West were being opened to all the riches of Eastern culture, the terms of trade were reversed between the hitherto undeveloped economies of Europe and the mature civilizations of China, Japan, and India. In 1814 the first shipment of cotton piece goods left Lancashire for Calcutta, leading in the course of a hundred years to the generation of a huge market for manufactured products. The astonishing Chinese appetite for opium was satisfied by smuggling into the country supplies of the drug grown in India, and China tea and silks were accompanied to the European market by indigo, jute, rice, and raw cotton from India. So the scope of trade between East and West, which had been largely a one-way traffic in luxury commodities paid for in bullion, developed after 1820 into a bustling intercourse.

Unprecedented economic expansion took place in the 1850s, fueled by the discovery of gold in California and Australia and the cultivation of wool, sugar, and coffee in Australia, South Africa, and Ceylon. The invention of the compound steam engine dramatically reduced the cost of shipping goods by sea, and, at the same time, the shortening of the sea route to India, coupled with inauguration of submarine cable links, helped to accelerate the growth of commerce. From 1880 refrigeration began to make it practicable to ship beef, lamb, butter, and fruit halfway around the globe.

Worldwide trade ballooned in the second half of the nineteenth century, and the opening of the Suez Canal in 1869 had the effect of channeling much of the resultant shipping through the Middle East. Britain had become embraced in an economic partnership with India which imbued every aspect of national life: industrial, social, military, cultural, and scientific. England, without India, was unthinkable, and the essential connection was an uninterrupted procession of steamships passing through the Canal.

In the days of sail, if you went to work for the East India Company you could expect to return home perhaps once before retirement; it was customary to grant a three-year furlough in mid-career. The voyage from England to India via the Cape of Good Hope took six months at least, and you might have another three or four months of traveling to do before reaching your final destination. Replies to letters, therefore, could well take over a year and a half to receive.

The technology of steam was the driving force behind the Industrial Revolution, and it was the introduction of steam propulsion that made possible regular transit of the Red Sea. Early steamers were grossly uneconomical; they were used first, therefore, in situations where passage under sail was most severely handicapped, as on canals, rivers, and lakes. The Red Sea is narrow, with treacherous shoals along its eastern shore, and prevailing winds blow in opposite directions in the northern half and in the south. It was not practical to operate from end-to-end on a regular basis under sail.

Before 1830 passengers bound for the East had no alternative to circumnavigating Africa. In that year the East India Company pioneered the Red Sea route with a small steamer, built in India, called the *Hugh Lindsay*. From 1835 the mails for India were sent through the Middle East rather than around the Cape, and in 1837, the Company started a steam packet service between Bombay and Suez with the paddlers *Berenice* and *Atalanta*. These early steamers were not equal to the task of maintaining their timetables throughout the monsoon, but the average journey time from India to Britain was reduced from six months to two.

The connection across the Middle East was suitable only for passengers and mail. There was an awkward trip by horse-drawn wagon 84 miles across the desert from Suez to Cairo, down the Nile in the *Jack O'Lantern*, a tiny paddle

Madras, the waterfront, 1860.
Madras had nothing in the way of protection for shipping until the
breakwater creating an artificial harbor was completed in 1910.

steamer, and then transit by barge on the Mahmoudieh Canal to the Mediterranean port of Alexandria. In 1840 the Peninsular and Oriental Steam Navigation Company won a contract to take over the packet service from there to England, hitherto run by the Admiralty. The whole journey was first described as the Steam Route; later, and more generally, it became known as the Overland Route.

Within three more years, P & O opened a regular steamer service from Suez to Calcutta via Ceylon and Madras. The obstacles were considerable: steam coal from South Wales had to be shipped to the Indian Ocean via the Cape, and by the 1850s, P & O alone employed some 170 sailing colliers for the purpose. Coal was stocked at Aden, roughly midway on the 3,000-mile voyage between Suez and Bombay; up to a third of the journey time was taken up in coaling ship.

A herd of 3,500 camels was employed in humping coal across the desert. The beasts were superseded in 1858 when the newly opened railway connecting Alexandria with Suez presented an alternative.

The East India Company had looked at other options. In 1834 they took part in an official expedition which employed two prefabricated iron steamers to explore the possibility of navigation down the length of the River Euphrates, but still the overland connection between Antioch and Aleppo was fraught with danger as well as with topographical and political obstacles. A railway from the Bosphorus to Baghdad was another enterprise which many considered would eventually lead to the most satisfactory route to India. This project was fraught with so many difficulties that the first train to complete the journey did not do so until 1940.

This was not the only railway scheme. During the course of the 1880s, the Russians pushed a line eastwards from the Caspian as far as Tajikistan, with dreams of penetrating the Himalayas and descending on the Indian Empire from the north. Later, the British squandered great effort on the construction of a railway westwards from India, through the Bolan Pass, and from there to the Persian border, with the idea of continuing on to Mesopotamia.

But it was left to a French entrepreneur to create a canal linking the

Mediterranean with the sea routes to the East. Ferdinand de Lesseps, after years of frustrating negotiation, succeeded in 1859 in obtaining a concession from the Khedive of Egypt. This was eventually sanctioned, albeit with grave misgivings, by his suzerain the Sultan. The canal was to be dug through the desert at its narrowest waist, from the delta of the Nile to the northern tip of the Red Sea at Suez. The capital was raised in France.

Making use of the Bitter Lakes which lay midway along the route, de Lesseps cut his waterway at sea level, without locks. Fortunately the Red Sea defied the prediction of Napoleon's chief engineer and failed to drain itself into the Mediterranean. The Suez Canal is 90 miles long and took ten years to build, but once it was opened, it began to attract the great bulk of traffic between East and West. Much of the trade to Australia and East Africa as well as that destined for India and the Far East was diverted through Suez, for the Middle East route was now no longer limited to passengers and high-value commodities such as spice, silk, and specie.

The Canal was opened to traffic at a moment when steam propulsion had just become competitive with sail for the shipping of bulk cargo. Adoption of the compound engine, coupled with higher steam pressures derived from better boilers, had tipped the scales. It is striking that in 1853, out of a total of 10,000 ships on Lloyds' Register, only 187 were steamers.[1] After 1869 the sailing ship was rapidly displaced on the Passage East, and by the end of the century between four and five thousand ships a year were passing through the Canal. All were steamships, and seven out of ten were British.

In the days before the Canal, mail for India would leave London by train, cross the Channel by ferry, and then continue by rail again across France to Marseilles, where it would be put aboard the P & O steamer. Passengers who could afford to do so traveled the same route, saving at least a week and avoiding the notorious swells and rollers of the Bay of Biscay. This route was briefly interrupted in 1870 by fighting in the Franco-Prussian War, but subsequently the new Mont Cenis railway tunnel through the Alps enabled the Indian Mail to switch its terminal to Venice. P & O started a shuttle service from there to Port Said, at the mouth of the Canal, where passengers and mail could now be

Bombay, the Taj Mahal Hotel, built on the Apollo Bunder in 1903.

[1] The Register included only ships insured at Lloyds, but at this time some of the major shipping lines carried their own insurance. Nevertheless, the relative numbers in sail and steam are remarkable.

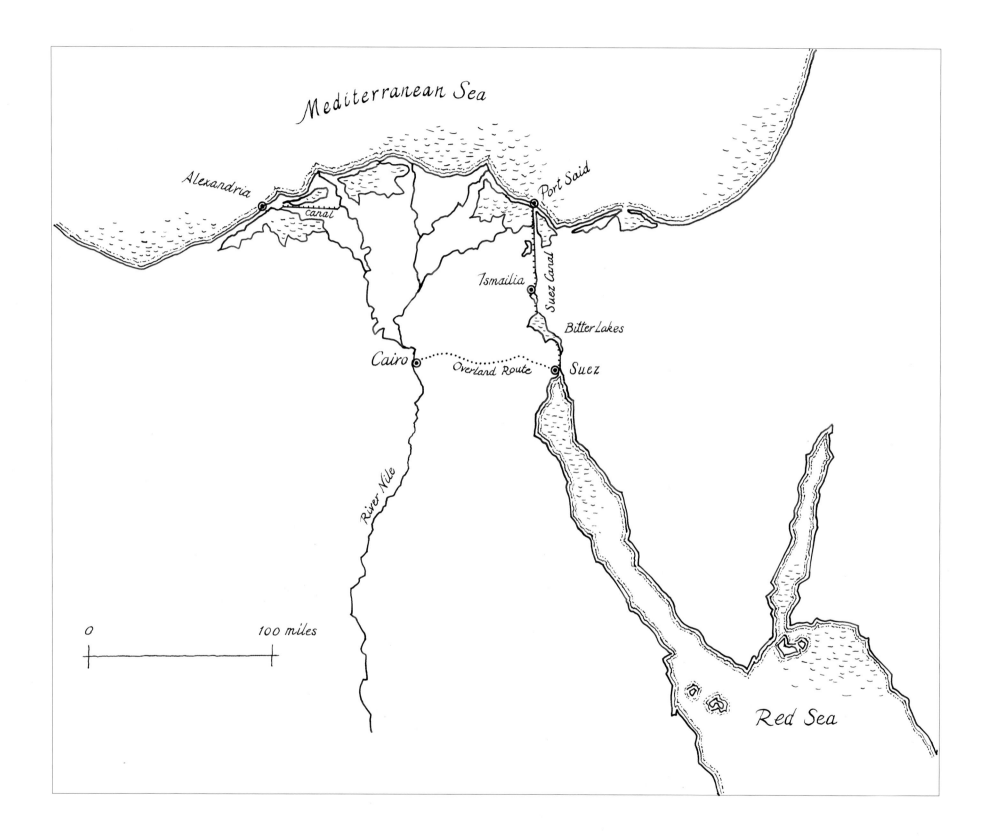

Wicker chairs and warmer weather on deck, 1910.

transferred straight onto the ship which would be taking them all the way to the East. Later, the rail connection was extended down the length of Italy to Brindisi, and this remained the itinerary until 1914. By this date the passage by ship all the way from London to Bombay was down to less than three weeks.

Back in the eighteenth century, news of the outbreak of war in Europe had been carried to India via the overland route. This enabled British forces there to steal a march on French garrisons at the start of the Seven Years' War. In 1798 intelligence of Napoleon's thunderstroke in Egypt reached Calcutta well before Nelson's dispatches arrived in London. Over the years, apprehensions over French intentions towards India were gradually replaced by perception of the growing threat from Russia. Military expansion by Czarist Russia towards the Straits of Bosphorus and the Mediterranean was countered by British support for the waning Ottoman Empire on three distinct occasions during the second half of the nineteenth century. Russian encroachment southward and eastward into the Khanates of Central Asia continued sporadically until 1904; in the course of the century the Russian Empire was brought as much as 2,000 miles closer to the

frontiers of British India, and the British had good reason never to be at ease about their further intentions.

Once the canal became a reality, therefore, British fear that the French might use it against British interests was replaced by recognition of its strategic as well as its commercial value to Britain. Within a couple of years, British troops were passing through at the rate of 35,000 a year. Concern for possible interference led to Disraeli's purchase of the Khedive's block of shares in the French Suez Company and to ever deeper British involvement in Egyptian affairs. The Canal proved to be of great benefit for the passage of troops in the First World War, and a Turkish attempt to interdict this traffic was repulsed. In the Second World War a determined attempt by the Axis to seize the canal was fought off at enormous cost. Security of the Canal remained a sensitive matter right up to the day when it was nationalized by President Abdel Nasser in 1956.

The age of steam was prolonged by the introduction of turbine propulsion in the early 1900s and then by oil-fired boilers, but the compression-ignition engine invented by Dr. Rudolf Diesel in 1897 gradually came into widespread

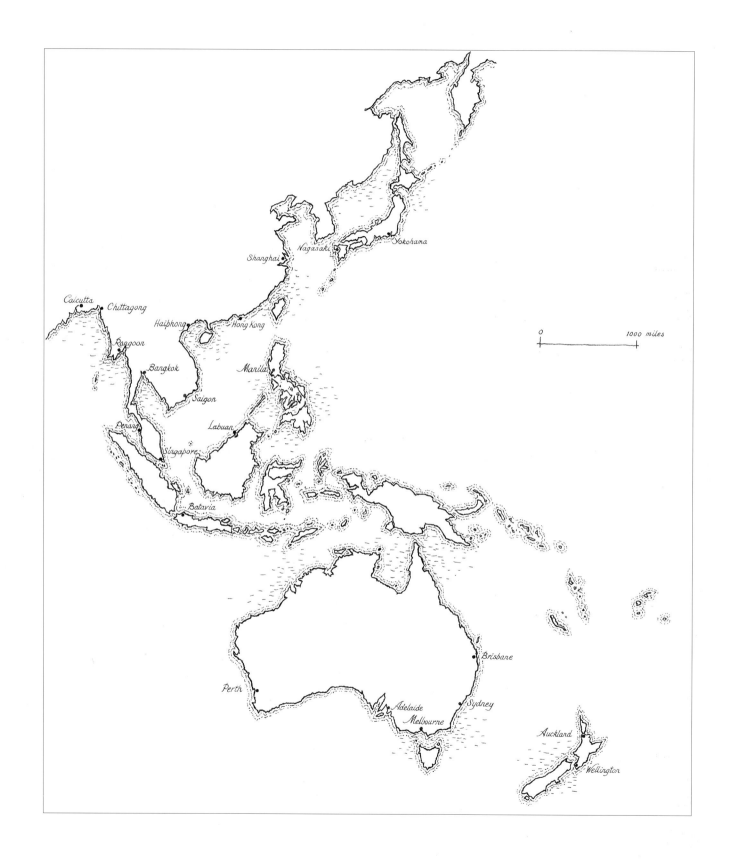

Calcutta Chittagong Haiphong Hong Kong Rangoon Bangkok Manila Saigon Penang Labuan Singapore Batavia Shanghai Nagasaki Yokohama Brisbane Perth Adelaide Sydney Melbourne Auckland Wellington

0 1000 miles

The town of Suez, with a small paddle steamer just discernible alongside.
The ship dates from the 1860s.

use during the second quarter of the twentieth century. The same 25-year period saw the evolution of airships, flying boats, and eventually of airliners to the stage of being able to carry mail and passengers reliably, and far more rapidly than ships. No more ships were built as passenger liners after 1968, and thereafter the use of steam propulsion in new construction was rare. So the extinction of scheduled passenger ship services on long-distance routes coincided with the decline of steam.

Political ties between India and Britain were terminated in 1947, and culturally as well as economically, the relationship between the mother country and her dependencies East of Suez withered in the following twenty years. The last sailing of a P & O passenger liner, the *Chusan*, took place from Bombay in February 1970. In retrospect, that year can be identified as the end of an era which commenced in 1837 with the opening of the service from Bombay to Suez by the steamer *Berenice*.

Plate 1.

HEICoS *Berenice,* Suez, 1837

In this picture we see the opening of a new trade route. In 1837 the Honourable East India Company started a scheduled steamer service between Bombay and Suez, at the head of the Red Sea, which marked the beginning of an era in east-west trade. For the first time, passengers and mail bound for India could go directly via the Middle East instead of undertaking the long, unpredictable journey around Africa. The journey time from London to Bombay was clipped from an uncertain six months or so to a matter of nine weeks.

Only steam power could make this possible. The Red Sea presents serious obstacles to regular transit under sail. It is narrow, the coastlines are fringed with shoals, and the regime of prevailing winds conspires to frustrate passage for extended periods of the year. Even the early steamers, which were under 800 tons and 250 horsepower, proved unable to keep to their timetables during the monsoons, and breakdowns were not infrequent.

The East India Company was a pioneer in steam propulsion which had been in use since about 1823, first on the Hooghly River, and then on the Ganges, the Brahmaputra, the Irrawaddy, and the Indus. At this stage, seagoing steamships were far from commercially viable, but in the absence of telegraph, the value to the administration in India of fast and regular communication was worth a subsidy, even though it included an awkward overland connection across Egypt.

The French and the British Governments were already operating steam packet services through the Mediterranean as far as Alexandria when the East India Company, in 1835, decided to order two paddlers for the Bombay-to-Suez run. *Atalanta* was built in London and *Berenice* in Glasgow, and both ships were launched in the following year. *Berenice,* which took three months on her maiden voyage around the Cape of Good Hope, measured 756 tons gross, carried a battery of 8-inch cannon, and was driven at 8 knots by her 220 hp engines.

Here she is portrayed on arrival for the first time at Suez, thrusting her way amongst the indigenous sailing craft which would eventually be eclipsed by the growing use of steam propulsion. The ensign which can be seen at her mainmast gaff is that of the Indian Marine, the navy of the East India Company; it resembles the Stars and Stripes but with the Union Jack in place of stars in the first quarter.

Plate 2.

PS *Euxine*, Southampton, 1848

The Peninsular and Oriental, from the start, announced itself as a Steam Navigation Company. This terminology later became conventional, but in 1837 it was significant: the company employed no sailing ships.

The little *Euxine* (1,100 tons) was launched on the Clyde in 1847, designed for service to Constantinople. (The Black Sea is the Latin *Pontus Euxinus*.) Passengers for the East would disembark at Alexandria for the overland crossing to Suez, where they would pick up another steamship to continue the voyage East. Thus the journey to India via the Middle East first became known as the Steam Route. The introduction of steam had made it possible to start regular services through the Red Sea from 1837, and in 1840, the P & O secured the mail contract between England and Egypt. Three years later, P & O steamers began carrying the mails between Suez and Calcutta, and by 1845, they extended the service to Singapore and Hong Kong.

Under the beneficial influence of the Isle of Wight, the port of Southampton enjoys four periods of high water in 24 hours. Following the completion of the London and South Western Railway in 1840, P & O moved its operations from London to Southampton. The South Western Hotel still stands at the terminus of the railway on Canute Road (since 1940 it has been used for shipping offices). Together with many of the smaller buildings that can be seen in the painting, they miraculously escaped bombing in the Second World War. An extensive area of docks and wharves now exists on reclaimed land stretching downriver, and railway tracks debouch across the road next to the hotel providing direct rail access to the docks. P & O continued to use Southampton until 1881, returning to the port only in the 1960s.

Euxine was an iron paddle steamer, 223 feet long, with accommodation for 80 First Class and 18 Second Class passengers and 443 tons of cargo. She had direct-acting two-cylinder oscillating engines manufactured by the shipbuilder, Caird & Co. of Greenock.

PS is the designation for Paddle Steamer. Screw Steamers were given the prefix SS. A ship engaged in carrying out a mail contract for the British Government was entitled to the description Royal Mail Ship, or RMS.

Plate 3.

Charing Cross Station, London, 1864

If you could afford to travel by the fastest route, along with the mails, the journey to India would start from London with a train on the South Eastern Railway which took you as far as Folkestone. This would be followed by the Channel crossing on board a steam packet to Boulogne, by train to Marseilles (preferably by Wagon-Lits), and then by the P & O steamer service to Alexandria. In the early years you would there embark on the Mahmoudieh Canal in a barge towed by horses, or from 1842, by a steam tug, and the journey up the Nile to Boulac, the port of Cairo, would be by means of a small river steamer, followed by an overnight stay at Shepheard's. You then had two alternatives. The first option was overland by horse-drawn wagon in eight stages across some 80 miles of desert to Suez, a journey usually undertaken at night but nevertheless notoriously uncomfortable. The second option, also organized by the ubiquitous Thomas Waghorn, was a sightseeing expedition up the Nile to Luxor followed by a much longer desert crossing to Kosseir on the Red Sea.

From 1856 it became possible to travel from Alexandria to Cairo by rail, and two years later saw the completion of the railway line from there to Suez. Finally, the whole journey could be done under steam.

The steamer service from Suez to Bombay was operated until 1854 by the East India Company, but thereafter was taken over by the P & O, which had already been operating the mail service to Ceylon and Calcutta for twelve years. So from Suez or Kosseir, at least, you had an unbroken voyage in the same ship, stopping inevitably for coaling at Aden, and landing finally in Bombay or at Point de Galle in Ceylon.

The Indian Mutiny took place in 1857. The news reached England via Suez in 30 days, but the authorities were reluctant to use the Overland Route for sending out troops partly, it was said, for fear of creating a precedent for its use by France. Reinforcements were shipped to India from South Africa, Mauritius, and Ceylon. Troops sent from England took 80 days to reach Calcutta via the Cape.

From 1844 the South Eastern Railway started at London Bridge Station, south of the river. Later the line was extended westward, across the Thames via Hungerford Bridge, and in 1864, a new terminus was opened at Charing Cross Station on the Strand. Until 1920 this was the principal point of departure for travelers bound for Europe; after that it became Victoria Station and recently, with the opening of the Channel Tunnel, it has become Waterloo.

Plate 4.

The French Imperial Yacht *L'Aigle* at the Opening of the Suez Canal, 8:30 A.M., November 18, 1869

Ismail Pasha, Khedive of Egypt, owed allegiance to the Sultan of Turkey. He decided to try to use the occasion of the opening of the Suez Canal to gain international recognition of full sovereignty for Egypt. The Sultan himself was not invited and let it be known that attendance by a foreign head of state would not be well received.

Ferdinand de Lesseps, creator of the Canal, was a nephew of Eugénie, consort of Napoleon III and Empress of France. It was thus the superb French imperial yacht *L'Aigle*, without the Emperor aboard, which led the procession of 46 ships southward through the Canal on the day of its opening. A pair of giant wooden obelisks was erected to mark the occasion.

The second ship to enter the canal was the Khedive's Yacht, *Mahroussa*. An iron-built paddle steamer constructed on the Thames in 1865, she was converted to turbine screw propulsion in Scotland in 1904. Astonishingly, this historic vessel is still in seagoing condition and in use as the Presidential Yacht.

Much modified and renamed *El Horria*, she can be found to this day among the Egyptian Navy ships moored within the mole at Alexandria.

The third ship to enter the canal that morning was the Austrian Imperial Yacht *Grief*, defiantly flying the ensign of the Emperor Franz Josef. The Crown Princes of Prussia and of Holland followed in her wake. The British government cautiously sent instructions to the Ambassador at Constantinople to attend the affair on board his dispatch boat *Psyche*.

From Suez three Egyptian gunboats steamed northward to meet the ceremonial flotilla in the Bitter Lakes. One of them ran firmly aground and was only with difficulty refloated to allow passage to the other ships. The P & O liner *Delta* arrived unannounced at Port Said so she was allocated last place in the proceedings. Consequently she was too late in arriving at Ismailia to allow her passengers to attend the inaugural ball which turned out to be, at the same time, extravagant and chaotic.

Plate 5.

RMS *Australia* and HMS *Iron Duke*, Aden, 1871

Posted to the China station in 1871, HMS *Iron Duke* became the first Royal Navy ironclad to make a transit of the Suez Canal. She drew nearly 23 feet and had to be towed through the waterway over a period of three days, grounding several times.

The P & O company was cautious. Months after its opening in November 1869, the Chairman pronounced the Canal not yet in a fit state for regular use, but in July 1870, *Delhi* was the first P & O ship to make a round trip to the East via Suez. In September, *Australia* made her maiden voyage via the Canal and on her return passage she carried a particularly urgent and valuable cargo—China tea. This shipment spelled the eclipse of the lovely square-rigged sailing clippers which used to compete in the great annual race around the Cape with the first of the new season's crop.

Compound expansion engines had been developed by John Elder of Glasgow in 1854. Improved metallurgy and boiler design enabled steam to be supplied at higher pressures, and the steam was led through two cylinders in succession. Later it became normal to have three cylinders in series, hence the term triple-expansion. Engines which reused the same steam in this way led to a reduction in coal consumption by as much as 50 percent, and this clinched the commercial advantage of steam over sail. The P & O tried them first in *Mooltan* in 1861, and after 1869 no new tonnage was ordered without. *Australia* had compound engines, and from 1870 to 1873, much of the company's fleet was converted.

Iron Duke and *Australia* are portrayed at Aden, the inevitable stop for bunkering. All sources agree as to the inhospitable nature of the place: crowded in by scorching red cliffs, the tiny peninsula bakes, as it were, in an oven. But Aden's importance was entirely a matter of location. Accessible by colliers under sail, whereas they would have had difficulty working up the Red Sea, it lay halfway between Suez and Bombay. From there, shipping lanes diverged in all directions across the Indian Ocean.

The hostile mountains of the Arabian interior descend in a chaos of precipices and defiles. Visitors would be taken to see the great water catchment works, but the reservoir was often dry and P & O was obliged to set up a coal-fired plant for desalinization of seawater.

The P & O saltwater distillation plant, Aden, c. 1875.

Plate 6.

RMS *Massilia*, Venice, 1872

One of the last paddle steamers built for P & O, *Massilia* was first employed on the Southampton-Alexandria route. She was an iron ship of 1,600 tons built on the Thames in 1860 and had two-cylinder oscillating engines which propelled her at 14 knots. She carried 140 passengers, and some would say that she and her contemporaries were the most beautiful ships to sail under the company flag.

The use of sail combined with steam goes far to explain the decline of paddlers in favor of screw propulsion. A paddle steamer under sail is inclined to find one wheel too deeply immersed while the other can barely bite the water, and the problem of drag when not under power is more difficult to overcome than with a screw.

Soon after P & O started sending its liners all the way to India through the Suez Canal, it inaugurated a branch service from Venice to Port Said. This enabled passengers to travel on the same train as the mail across Europe, board the *Massilia* or one of her consorts at Venice, and catch up with their main ship either at Malta or in Egypt. In 1898 this route was superseded by a shuttle service between Brindisi and Port Said operated by a pair of small, fast vessels specially built for the purpose and named *Osiris* and *Isis*.

Massilia is the ancient Greek name for Marseilles, a port of call on her original itinerary.

Marseilles, Le Vieux Port, c. 1870.

Plate 7.

RMS *Peshawur,* the Upper Deck, 1872

Built in 1871, the *Peshawur* was an iron screw steamer with compound engines designed for the Bombay service via the Canal. In 1882 she collided with an unlit sailing vessel off Ceylon while taking the English Test Cricket team to Australia. There was consternation because the English fast bowler F. Morley was severely injured.

Liners of the period carried slight superstructure above the main deck. White canvas was stretched over a kind of pergola to provide shade once the ship reached warm waters.

Passengers on the P & O consisted largely of public officials and military men. There would be a coterie of planters, no doubt, a leavening of businessmen, and a clutch of earnest missionaries, at least one of whom would inevitably be eager to enlighten a captive audience, but the great majority of passengers to India were on official duty.

The elite were covenanted members of the Indian Civil Service, the administrative corps which ran the country. Astonishingly, at no time throughout the period of British rule did the I.C.S. include more than 1,000 Britons. Passengers included army officers (the troops generally traveled en masse by troopship), doctors and surveyors, judges and foresters, policemen, engineers, and accountants.

Cadets on their first tour would invariably travel single, but many of the other passengers would be making the journey *en famille*. Young ladies, suitably chaperoned, would take the passage to India in order to visit papa, a brother, or perhaps a cousin. Roguishly, they were collectively termed the "fishing fleet."

For all those on board, the inevitable period of idleness coupled with daily close quarters was a valuable interlude for "making contacts" and "learning the ropes."

Setting out for an afternoon drive.

Plate 8.

SS *Ethiopia*, Zanzibar, 1875

Lighthouse towers were sometimes built in the very midst of a town in order to guide approaching shipping to the port. Madras erected one such lighthouse, followed by Port Said and Colombo. In the same way, a lighthouse was built in the middle of the town of Zanzibar, on the waterfront adjoining the Sultan's Palace. Later it was incorporated into the structure of the Bet-el-Ajaib, the principal government building, which today is endearingly described as the House of Wonders.

This view of the British India Steam Navigation Company's *Ethiopia* is seen from the top of the lighthouse, looking down over the port area at the northern end of the Stone Town. Zanzibar at this time was the only place of consequence on the coast of East Africa, and the various expeditions which set out to explore the Interior started there by hiring porters before crossing to the mainland at Bagomoyo.

The island, which is almost within sight of the coast of Africa, was an Arab colony. The annual cycle of the monsoons, southwest followed by northeast, facilitated a regular, if leisurely, trade by *dhow* across the Arabian Sea. In 1840 Seyyid Said, Sultan of Oman, transferred his capital from Muscat to Zanzibar.

British interest in Zanzibar arose through efforts to suppress the Indian Ocean slave trade, and from 1821, treaties were negotiated with Seyyid Said to try to bring this abominable traffic to an end. When he died in 1856, the Sultan's inheritance was divided, one son becoming ruler of Oman and another of Zanzibar. The Royal Navy intercepted an Omani fleet bent on seizing Zanzibar in order to revive the export of slaves. Thereafter, Britain found herself effectively the protector of Zanzibar, whose independence was threatened first by France and later by Germany. The principal personality was Dr. (later Sir John) Kirk, who for over 20 years served as British Consul-General and became friend and adviser to two successive Sultans. He was a long-standing associate of Dr. David Livingstone.

The island was, throughout the nineteenth century, the principal world source of cloves, and it became the center of a prosperous entrepôt trade embracing mainland Africa, the Arabian Gulf, India, and Western trading nations including the United States.

The British India company introduced regular services from Aden and other ports up and down the coast in 1873. Evidently the Sultan was impressed by its style of management, for in 1877, he invited the chairman, Sir William Mackinnon, to take charge of Zanzibar's extensive mainland territories, over which he exercised a somewhat shaky authority, and to administer and develop them on his behalf. The offer was courteously declined.

Zanzibar, the lighthouse and the Sultan's Palace, c. 1875.

Deck scene, HMT Serapis, *1875.*

Plate 9.

HMT *Malabar* in the Suez Canal, 1875

Many accounts describe the curious sight of an oceangoing ship apparently plowing through the sand. Her Majesty's Indian Troopship *Malabar* is here seen carrying a draft of fresh recruits southward on their way to fill the ranks of battalions depleted, no doubt, largely by malaria. On April 8, 1875, the troops on board spotted Ferdinand de Lesseps himself on horseback by Lake Timsah. They lined the rails and gave three rousing cheers.

In November 1875 the *Malabar* was instructed to call at Alexandria on her return voyage from India. There she picked up seven zinc trunks containing 177,606 shares in the Suez Canal Company which had been deftly purchased for the British government by Disraeli. The shares were the portion of stock held by the Khedive of Egypt, who received for them the sum of £ 3,976,582. They were safely transferred to the Bank of England before the end of the year. The deal was popularly regarded as a great coup.

After 30 years of service as a trooper, the *Malabar* ended her days as an accommodation ship at Ireland Island dockyard in Bermuda. She was stationed there from 1897 to 1919 and gave her name to the naval shore establishment on the island.

Plate 10.

SS *Bokhara* and *Nepaul*, Hong Kong, 1879

The scene around the roadstead, sheltered from the South China Sea by Hong Kong Island, has changed since 1879 as drastically as any place on earth. The shoreline has encroached into the harbor and the town of Victoria (or Central) now presents a glittering phalanx of mirror-glass facades jostling one another for attention.

In 1879 the waterfront was lined with urbane, arcaded buildings of two to three stories, and the architecture of the Naval Dockyard had a certain air of measured elegance. The harbor bustled with merchant ships loading or discharging cargoes destined for godowns along the shore. Much in evidence were Chinese junks and sampans, ships' boats under oar, a side-wheel paddle tug, and the R.N. Receiving Ship HMS *Victor Emmanuel.* This vessel, a wooden screw-driven ship of the line built in 1855 as HMS *Repulse,* had been roofed-over and served for twenty years as the naval headquarters and accommodation ship.

The Chinese craft to be seen in the harbor comprised a range of traditional, specialized types of great sophistication in design and construction. They were vessels of delicate beauty; such craft have largely been superseded by debased modern versions.

In the center of the painting are two P & O liners, *Bokhara* and *Nepaul.* *Bokhara* was an iron ship of 3,000 tons, built, as were so many ships for P & O, by Caird's of Greenock on the lower Clyde. Completed in 1873, she carried 200 passengers and her compound engines gave her a service speed of 12 knots. *Nepaul,* 500 tons larger, was built in 1876. She was faster (14 knots) but carried only 140 passengers.

Note that both ships are employing their yards as derricks in the process of loading. The *Nepaul* is badly out of trim in the process; before weighing anchor she will, of course, be brought to an even keel.

Hong Kong, the Club, c. 1870.

Plate 11.

The Suez Canal Company Offices, Port Said, 1879

The headquarters of the Suez Canal Company in Port Said comprised a fanciful triple-domed building behind which lay the company's warehouses and workshops. Adjoining is the Commercial basin in which can be seen the dredgers, lighters, and pilot tenders required to maintain the canal in working order. Beyond lies the Ismail basin and the entrance to the canal.

Ships were obliged to moor at Port Said and wait for a southbound convoy to be cleared for transit. For many years passage was not allowed after dark. Pilots were essential, and the job acquired a certain mystique. When Colonel Gamal Abdel Nasser seized the canal in 1956, the French and British pilots went on strike, supposing that all traffic would be brought to a standstill, but the Egyptians proved perfectly capable of keeping things moving.

When the canal was first opened, there was concern that it would provide a channel for the transmission of epidemics such as bubonic plague and cholera. Northbound shipping had to pass inspection by the *Cordon Sanitaire*.

The canal is not a straight cut; there are eighteen changes of direction, and in the early days, ships used to be fitted with an auxiliary rudder to augment steerage during transit. Although the waterway had a minimum width of 500 feet on the surface, the dredged channel was only 72 feet wide at the bottom. The designed depth was to have been 26 feet, but at the inauguration the available draught was no more than 13 feet in places, and grounding was a frequent occurrence.

The canal has been widened and deepened several times over the years, but it is still the practice to "cat the anchor" on very large ships, holding it ready to drop instantly in the event of losing control.

Plate 12.

RMS *Ancona* at Shanghai, 1880

Lying at moorings in the Huangpu River, opposite the Shanghai Club, the P & O steamer *Ancona* is engaged in discharging cargo into lighters alongside. She is riding high and, therefore, her holds are probably nearly empty.

The *Ancona* is representative of a large number of very similar ships that were built for P & O during the 1870s. She was launched by Caird and Co. in 1879 and employed on the service from London to the Far East. She was iron-built, of 3,080 gross registered tonnage, with a two-cylinder inverted compound engine manufactured by the shipbuilder. Her service speed was 12.5 knots, and she carried 184 passengers.

Shanghai was one of five Treaty Ports designated in the Treaty of Nanking in 1842 where the British, seen as troublesome as well as uncivilized, were reluctantly to be allowed to live and to conduct trade. They were allocated an area on the left bank of the Huangpu, downstream from the old Chinese city and about 15 miles from the point where that river enters the estuary of the mighty Yangtse-kiang. The Yangtse, which is ten miles wide when it discharges its load of yellow mud into the East China Sea, is navigable for some 1,400 miles upriver through the heartland of China.

The British were joined by other nationalities in what became the International Settlement. They built an embankment to contain the Huangpu from flooding, on top of which was laid out a broad road lined with trees. This was called the Bund, and along it were constructed the principal foreign buildings, the consulates, the banks, commercial offices, hotels, and clubs.

The word "bund" was commonly used in India to describe any dyke or river embankment, but in the case of Shanghai, the term became world-famous.

Chinese junks.

Plate 13.

HMT *Euphrates*, Port Said, 1881

In 1866 five great, white troopships were built for the Government of India, each of which could accommodate an entire battalion of troops and their equipment. The ships plied to and fro between Britain and India for nearly thirty years until the policy was changed to that of chartering liners for the purpose. The Bibby Line, whose ships were named for English counties, came to specialize in this business, but other shipping lines also built ships designed for trooping and provided ships under charter from time to time. In time of war almost all the passenger ships engaged in the Eastern trade were pressed into military service, as troopships, hospital ships, or armed merchant cruisers.

The *Euphrates* is moored opposite the lighthouse at Port Said, headed south for the Red Sea and the Indian Ocean. Her sister ships were called *Serapis*, *Crocodile*, *Jumna*, and *Malabar* (see Plate 9). Before the opening of the Canal in 1869, two of the troopers operated as far as Alexandria and the others between Suez and Bombay. Their soldiers were carried across Egypt by train.

The northern stretch of the Suez Canal was constructed by dredging through shallow water rather than by cutting through desert, and the entrance, where it penetrated the sandy rim of the Delta, had to be protected from silting-up by building a mole out into the sea. The first building to be erected was a lighthouse to guide shipping, and by 1881 not much of the city had yet grown up around this landmark.

The lighthouse at Port Said was inaugurated on March 20, 1870, and it became a signature of the place, much in the same way as have Brooklyn Bridge, Tower Bridge, and the Eiffel Tower.

Plate 14.

SS *Goorkha* in the Hooghly, 1882

Up to the end of the 1880s, it was normal practice to use sail to augment steam power on long-distance routes, and thereby to improve economy. Steam was essential for keeping to a timetable, but it never became competitive with sail for carrying bulk cargo until about 1865, and the use of sail by no means stopped abruptly. During the following 25 years there was worthwhile scope for saving coal—and occasionally for increasing speed or steadying the ship—by exploiting the available wind. Sailing rig was not a sign of incorrigible conservatism, nor was it only a prudent precaution against breakdowns, but it was a carefully designed component of a steamship, and it was put to everyday use.

Auxiliary steam in a full-rigged ship was rare, but sail-assisted steam was commonplace. A steamer would follow steamship routes as a matter of course, but once at sea she would hoist whatever sail best suited the conditions. Up until 1902, ships for the British India line were provided with gaff schooner rig although their broad beam and widely spaced masts enabled them to do without booms, and before 1894, foremasts were equipped with yards to carry square sails.

It is an interesting insight to trading conditions in the nineteenth century that BI ships were regularly run aground at minor ports of call where there was a gently shelving beach so that the vessel could be discharged and loaded before the ensuing flood tide. The screw acting in reverse would help to scour the sand from beneath the hull if departure had been delayed too long.

British India's SS *Goorkha* was one of a pair built in 1881 by William Denny & Brothers of Dumbarton, a firm which for many years built the lion's share of BI ships. The two firms had such a close association that the construction contract was written on no more than a single sheet of paper. She measured 4,000 tons, she had a single screw driven by a two-cylinder compound inverted oscillating engine, six boilers operating at 70 lbs, and the ship could make 11 knots under steam. She carried 115 passengers in first and second classes, and she was the first in the fleet with electric lighting. *Goorkha* had a service life of 25 years, which seems to have been a typical life-span for merchant ships throughout the age of steam.

The liner is seen near the end of a voyage from London, making her way up the Hooghly River to Calcutta under the charge of a pilot. In the foreground are the rice paddies of Bengal, tilled by water buffalo. "Country-boats" with square sail rig are still to be found throughout the Ganges delta, that great area of Bangladesh and West Bengal which is home to millions and is the scene of recurrent calamitous flooding. The landscape is strikingly reminiscent of Holland.

Plate 15.

RMS *Sutlej*, the Landing Stage at Ismailia, 1883

The old port of Suez at the head of the Red Sea, being isolated from the course of the new canal, was bypassed by modern shipping. The new town of Ismailia, which was established by the Canal Company to serve as its headquarters midway along the route, became the port of call. Homeward bound passengers who wanted to go ashore could travel from there to Cairo by train, take a sightseeing tour of the Pyramids, and rejoin their ship at Port Said or Alexandria.

Ismailia lies at the northern end of the Great Bitter Lakes. It was named by the Company for the Khedive Ismail Pasha who succeeded Said Pasha in 1863.

Here we see shipping accumulating to wait its turn in a northbound convoy for passage to Port Said. Tourists have been brought ashore in a rather spindly-looking paddle-driven tender and they're already being jostled by Egyptian touts.

Sutlej was a 4,200-ton P & O liner with room for 170 passengers. She was launched at Barrow in 1881 and was employed on the run to the Far East. In 1898 she attempted, without success, to refloat the battleship HMS *Victorious*, which had suffered the indignity of running aground in the Canal. The Navy extricated itself in due course.

Plate 16.

SS *Orient*, Colombo, 1883

The Fort at Colombo established by the Portuguese in 1518 was extended and consolidated by the Dutch after their landing in Ceylon a century later. But the principal port of the island was at Point de Galle, 70 miles further south, where there was a far better natural harbor. It was not until 1875, seventy years after Ceylon had become a British colony, that the foundations were laid for an artificial breakwater to create a sheltered roadstead at Colombo. At the same time, a lighthouse and clock tower was built in the center of the Fort.

The old Dutch fortifications of Colombo surrounded an island which was only a mile across. There were eight stone bastions and an outlying battery on the harbor side. The landward side was protected by Beira Lake, augmented by artificial inundations, and the approaches were by means of causeways. The modern capital of Sri Lanka is centered on this historic core.

In 1879 a new shipping company was formed to compete with P & O in the mail and passenger service to Australia. It was called the Orient Steam Navigation Company, and its first ship, appropriately named *Orient*, made her maiden voyage from London to Adelaide via the Cape in the record-breaking time of just over five weeks. The return journey was made by way of Colombo and the Suez Canal, and from 1883, the same route was followed for both outbound and homeward passages.

Orient was built by John Elder & Co. on the Clyde. Her tonnage was 5,400 gross, she carried 650 passengers, and had a service speed of 15 knots. On her trials she made 17 knots, a sensational speed in 1879. She was one of the first to be fitted for refrigerated cargo and with electric lighting. *Orient* was renovated and re-engined in 1897 and continued in service until 1910.

Colombo, building the breakwater, c. 1880.

Plate 17.

RMS *Victoria,* the Boat Deck, 1889

Completed by Caird's of Greenock in 1887, the P & O liner *Victoria* attended the Queen's Silver Jubilee Naval Review in the Solent that summer before commencing her maiden voyage to Sydney.

Of nearly 400 passengers on board, 230 traveled First Class, and it is they whom we see in this view, promenading on deck. Judging by the elaboration of the ladies' costumes, it may be the occasion of the Gala Dinner, two days out from Brisbane, for packing would commence the next day, and one was not expected to dress for dinner on the last night at sea.

Elements of interest are the broad white decks, scrubbed down every morning, the light structure of the navigating bridge with its emergency life belt, canvas awnings rigged for shade, deck lights open for ventilation, davits swung outboard, and rope netting tied to the rails to stop small children from climbing or articles of clothing from being blown overboard. In addition to the funnels, we see ventilators rising above the top of the deckhouse; the cowls swiveled and would tend to be left every which way to catch any available breeze.

Plate 18.

RMS *Arcadia,* Grand Harbour, Malta, 1889

Four elegant liners launched for the P & O in 1887, the fiftieth year of Queen Victoria's reign, were known as the Jubilee class. The first, of course, was named *Victoria* (see Plate 17) followed by *Britannia, Oceana,* and *Arcadia.* They were long and slender with two tall funnels and four masts. The ships had a gross tonnage of 6,500, a speed of 16 knots, and carried 400 passengers. The ratio of a liner's length to beam had generally been between seven and eight to one, but with ships designed to operate through the Suez Canal, this changed so that their length became nine times the beam or even greater. In some cases, ships were lengthened in order to reduce the draft, but there seems to have been also a vogue for longer, narrower hulls in pursuit of fuel economy.

An interesting detail which can be seen on a number of P & O ships at this period is the turtlebacked superstructure, not only at the bows but also near the stern of the ship, designed for shedding water which might break aboard. Note also the pair of curious little turrets on either side of the ship, just forward of the foremast, which accommodate the navigation lights.

Awnings were spread to shade the decks as soon as ships entered the Mediterranean on the outward voyage. Also evident in this view is the forest of ventilators for supplying fresh air, particularly needed to feed the furnaces in the boiler room. Breakdowns were not a remotely uncommon experience, and liners were still provided with sailing rig for emergencies: yards can be seen here on the two forward masts. The first twin-screw P & O did not make its appearance until 1896; after 1900 all new liners built for the company were so equipped and, therefore, could safely do without sails.

Malta was a long-standing port of call on the P & O route to the East. No setting could be more dramatic than Grand Harbour, the deep blue waters of which are surrounded by cliffs crowded with the lovely stone towns of Valetta, Floriana, Senglea, and Vittoriosa. It was the principal naval base in the Mediterranean, and the Royal Mail ships could lie at ease amongst the bluff ironclads of the Mediterranean Fleet.

Maltese dghaisas.

Plate 19.

RMS *Ophir*, Suez Canal, 1892

In 1891 a rakish, twin-screw liner called *Ophir* entered the mail service to Australia as flagship of the Orient Line. The engine room lay between two pairs of boiler rooms, hence the widely spaced funnels. She had triple-expansion engines which drove her at 18 knots, but she gained a reputation for extravagance in coal. Robert Napier & Co. of Glasgow were the shipbuilders, her gross registered tonnage was 6,800, and she had accommodation for nearly 900 passengers, 520 of them as immigrants.

In 1900 *Ophir* was chartered by the Admiralty to convey the Duke and Duchess of York (later King George V and Queen Mary) to Australia for the opening of the first Commonwealth Parliament. For the purpose of this journey, she was painted white and commissioned into the Navy as a Royal Yacht. After 1905 the Orient Line livery was changed from that depicted in the painting to black hull, white superstructure, and buff funnels.

During the First World War, *Ophir* served as an armed merchant cruiser and later as a hospital ship. She was sold in 1922.

One of the Suez Canal dredgers can be seen in the picture. They were steam-powered bucket dredgers, some with extending arms to enable them to discharge sand directly onto the banks of the canal. These craft had twin funnels, one on each side of a central structure which carried the endless chain of buckets. Some fifty such vessels were in use at the height of the construction period, together with hundreds of hopper barges to transport the spoil, great pumping dredgers, and a vessel specially designed for rock-cutting.

In the foreground is a wooden jetty serving one of the many cross-canal ferries.

Plate 20.

The Grand Hotel, Calcutta, 1893

The Grand Hotel on Chowringhee, Calcutta, must have been a well-known sight to old India hands returning from leave. Equally familiar, but less appealing, were the inevitable scavenging crows which still strut and squabble in the street.

Outside, in the oppressive steamy heat, waited the ricksha boys and dejected horses drooping in their traces. The hotel lobby was buried deep within the block, and to reach it, one passed down a long, dark corridor lined with shops.

The titles of the great hotels were resonant: the Grand Oriental in Colombo, the Taj Mahal in Bombay, Raffles in Singapore, Shepheard's in Cairo, the Peninsula in Hong Kong, and the Great Eastern along with the Grand in Calcutta. Personal service, no doubt, was discreet and attentive. Today's traveler would regard their physical comforts as primitive indeed, but those Victorians who could travel first class moved in a privileged world, insulated once they were inside the hotel from the distressing reality of life without. That much has not changed.

Grand Oriental Hotel, Colombo, c. 1890.

Plate 21.

HMS *Nile* and *Ramillies*, Grand Harbour, Malta, 1896

A portrait of the Passage East should include a painting of warships, for the whole tenuous thread of merchant shipping on which Britain depended was secured, in the last resort, by the existence of a great navy.

In order to be an effective deterrent, sea power had to be deployed, and throughout the period the Royal Navy maintained, in addition to home forces, a fleet in the Mediterranean and cruiser squadrons on the East Indies, the China, the South Atlantic and the North America-and-West Indies Stations.

From the date of its capture from the French in 1800, Malta became the principal overseas base of the Navy for it lay at the vortex of the worldwide pattern of Imperial trade routes. In the nineteenth century the most serious threat was seen to be likely to come from the French and later, from the Russians. Towards the end of the century, there loomed the prospect of having to contend with both their navies in combination.

In 1896 no fewer than twelve British battleships were stationed at Malta. They lay at their moorings in the superb setting of Grand Harbour, surrounded by creamy white limestone cliffs encrusted with the subtle geometry of fortifications devised in the sixteenth century by Italian military engineers working for the Knights of St. John.

The new battleship HMS *Ramillies*, seen in the right background, was flagship of Admiral Sir Michael Seymour. She was accompanied by her sister ship *Revenge* (only the stern of which is visible in the picture). The *Nile,* a turret ship of slightly earlier design, lies in the left foreground. The rest of the battle fleet consisted of the turret ships *Trafalgar* and *Hood*, together with older ships of the Admiral class.

All the battleships carried a main armament of four 13.5-inch guns—two forward and two aft; in most of the ships the guns were mounted in the open on armored barbettes. There was a substantial secondary armament of "quick-firing" 6-inch guns in casemates. The ships had a displacement of 10,000 to 14,000 tons, they were broad in the beam and protected by an armored belt of compound armor 14 inches to 18 inches thick. They also carried 3-inch deck armor at approximately the level of the waterline. The battleships had triple-expansion engines with coal-fired boilers, and with forced draught, they were capable of 15 to 17 knots.

The Admiralty tug Sampson *at Malta, 1902.*

Plate 22.

RMS *India* Beseiged by Bumboats, Port Said, 1897

A steamer picking up moorings in Port Said became the target for a converging rush of bumboats whose oarsmen would pester passengers to go ashore. There they would be subjected to the most unrelenting salesmanship, from vendors at street stalls and curio dealers to the most humble gully-gully man seeking largesse in return for his display of sleight of hand. Peddlers would clamor for attention, their wares consisting of fake antiques, brass trinkets, feathers, dried dates, and Turkish Delight. The whole object was to fleece the innocent traveler in the short time available.

Almost everybody who went ashore at Port Said paid a visit to the famous emporium of tropical gear and Eastern curios belonging to Simon Arzt.

On the eastern side of the channel lay the coaling depot. Great mounds of coal lay on the bank, and lighters would be made fast alongside the ship to transfer their loads into the bunkers on the port side (in a southbound ship) while passengers lined the rails to starboard.

The *India* was an 8,000-ton passenger liner which joined P & O in 1896; four similar ships, named *China , Egypt, Arabia,* and *Persia*, were built for the company before the end of the century. She carried 470 passengers, and her triple-expansion engines gave her a speed of 18 knots.

The statue of Ferdinand de Lesseps on the mole at Port Said.

Plate 23.

Awnings Rigged for the Red Sea,   1902

Transit of the Red Sea, whose narrow waters are constricted by mighty deserts, was seldom a comfortable experience. With a following wind, it was dreadful.

Awnings would be rigged along the sides of the upper deck, but nothing could be done to protect cabins situated along the sides of the ship on the decks below.

Heading southeast, cabins on the starboard side were exposed all through the afternoon to broiling sun striking more or less at right angles to black-painted hull plating. In smaller ships it was commonplace for passengers to abandon their bunks and bed-down in some segregated corner of the upper deck, in search of a breath of air. On the homeward voyage, conditions were reversed. Heading northwestward, it was cabins on the port side which lacked shade throughout the latter part of the day.

There is a familiar legend that seasoned travelers would call for reservations "Port Out, Starboard Home." In the shorthand of booking clerks, such passengers would be briefly annotated: "POSH." The dictionary lends little support to the story, merely recording that the word was first used in 1918, slang for smart or "swell."

The signaling station, Aden.

Plate 24.

Coaling ship, Aden, 1905

Coaling was a fact of life, grueling but inescapable. Coal heavers were employed to bring the fuel on board by the basketful, just as firemen and trimmers were needed for the arduous, skilled, but generally brutish, task of feeding the furnaces once a ship was at sea. Even in a world much more used than our own to hard physical labor, these were strenuous and sometimes dangerous jobs.

Coaling was often performed by Somalis who were considered to be best acclimatized to working in severe heat. Crew members recruited in the East were generally known as *lascars*, an Urdu word for seaman, and the greatest number of them came from Bengal.

In the scorching heat of Aden coaling was carried out, when possible, by night, but what made coaling ship a misery was the sticky-black, gritty, and pervasive nature of the material. Tipping coal raised choking clouds of dust. It got into the nose, eyes, and mouth, and it penetrated every nook and cranny of the ship.

Bunkering could take up to a third of the total round trip time of a voyage. Deepwater berths were seldom available outside home ports, so coal had to be brought off in lighters. Wooden ramps were rigged between the lighter and the sheer side of the ship, and coal would be shoveled into wicker baskets, carried up swaying ramps, and tipped into hatches in the side or on deck. A gang of forty coal heavers could coal ship at the rate of 30 tons an hour. Within, trimmers had to shovel in the darkness to distribute it throughout the bunkerage capacity. Men working in the bunkers had to be counted as they emerged and before coaling hatches were secured.

At Aden, much of the coal was stored in hulks, retired cargo ships which lay at moorings in Back Bay.

Note the detail of the ship's hull. Steel plates are riveted to the framing, butt jointed end-to-end but overlapped along top and bottom. One plate is half a deck in height, and it is either raised or suppressed relative to the adjoining strakes above and below, unlike the overlapping sequence of boards in wooden clinker-built construction.

Plate 25.

RMS *Malwa* in Plymouth Sound, 1910

From the end of 1881, mail ships of the P & O would put in to Plymouth Sound on the homeward voyage to allow passengers and mail to go ashore. There they could catch an afternoon express on the Great Western Railway. The ship would take at least another day to make her way up the Channel, wait for the tide to proceed up the Thames, and take her turn to pass through the locks in order to enter the docks at Tilbury before she could discharge her cargo. This is likely to have included such raw materials as teak, tea, rice, jute, rubber, and wool.

Returning expatriates are here being greeted by characteristic West Country weather. The rain has relented just enough to reveal Drake's Island on the left with the woods of Mount Edgcumbe beyond. Gaff-rigged fishing smacks are making their way back to Sutton Harbour, and there is a hint of naval traffic emerging from the Hamoaze. *Malwa*, having just dropped anchor, is blowing off a wisp of excess steam.

Seventh of the ten ships of the "M" class, *Malwa* was built on the Clyde in 1908. By standards of the North Atlantic such ships were neither large nor opulent. She had a registered tonnage of 11,000 gross, coal-fired boilers supplying vertical quadruple-expansion engines which gave her a speed of 18 knots, and she carried 600 passengers, 400 of whom were in First Class. *Malwa* operated between London and Sydney, only one among some 50 passenger liners in the P & O fleet at that time. In 1922 she carried my parents to Penang where my father had been posted to a branch of the Mercantile Bank of India.

The company livery consisted of sober black funnels above tan upperworks (officially described as "stone" colored), surmounting a black hull relieved by a white stripe. Some considered it dingy, but there are those who have always thought that nothing could be smarter. The color scheme was undoubtedly practical and could not remotely be regarded as ostentatious. It suited the P & O.

Plate 26.

SS *Perseus*, Calcutta, 1910

The Ocean Steam Shipping Company was registered in Liverpool in 1865, and was later known as Alfred Holt & Co. Ltd, or popularly as the Blue Funnel Line. The proprietor was a canny railway engineer who played a major role in the evolution and commercial application of the compound steam engine. It was this development which made steam-powered cargo ships a paying proposition. Holt was quick to appreciate the commercial significance of the Suez Canal, and the company prospered from the introduction of compound-engined freighters in the China trade as soon as it was opened. Such ships dealt a mortal blow to the age of sail.

Named for Greek classical heroes, Holt's ships were invariably conservative in appearance with a single gigantic funnel, bolt upright, a straight stem, and traditional counter stern. They were known also for their graceful sheer line. Blue Funnel ships were built to exceed the specifications required by Lloyd's for rating A1; Holt personally selected his captains and the company carried its own insurance.

Perseus is seen making her way downstream past the center of Calcutta, with the dome of the General Post Office in Dalhousie Square visible on the left and the Gothick outline of the High Court in the distance. Calcutta lies some 150 miles from the open sea on the Hooghly River, which is part of the enormous and bewildering combined delta system of the Ganges and Brahmaputra Rivers. Pilots on the Hooghly belonged to a celebrated *corps d'elite* whose knowledge of the treacherous seasonal changes in the watercourses and of the submerged and constantly shifting mudbanks was legendary.

The first of a class of nineteen 6,700-ton cargo liners, *Perseus* was built in 1908 with the three island type of hull typical in her day. She had a triple-expansion engine driving a single screw, supplied by two double-ended coal-fired boilers. Her operating speed was 14 knots, and she carried twelve passengers. Holt ships had unusually heavy derricks, and their hatches were extra large, enabling them to specialize in carrying large and heavy items such as locomotives.

A train on the Darjeeling Himalayan Railway.

Southampton, the Town Pier.

On Board

The Eastern Journey was like part of life, like the beginning of term, or the annual session with the dentist.

—Jan Morris

What it was like on board? This is the very kernel of the marine historian's task.

To start, let us compare passage east with its great geographical alternative, passage west, the transatlantic norm for millions of passengers. I first embarked on a liner in New York at the age of six months in 1930. Ever since, to my Scottish/American sensibilities, "abroad" meant "transatlantic." Moreover, passenger traffic on that ocean always represented the naval architectural big league.

Spanning the 3,000 miles of fractious North Atlantic separating old world from new demanded tonnage that was not only the largest but, concomitantly, the fastest and most splendid. Competition was fierce: shipowners wanted to attract both the cream of the fickle traveling public as well as the seemingly infinite numbers of westbound emigrants. As a result, huge, fast ships entered service, surpassing the speed and displacement of vessels anywhere else. At the time, for example, that White Star Line's 45,000-ton *Olympic* was conceived at Belfast's Harland & Wolff, P&O's *Mooltan* of 1905 displaced less than 10,000 tons. Lower demand for berthing space as well as the limitations of Suez's canal restricted the parameters of Far Eastern tonnage.

Then there was the contrasting duration of passenger tenancy. As transatlantic hulls grew, passage time was curtailed. In 1895, Cunard's *Lucania* thundered to New York in a record-breaking five days, seven hours. By the turn of the century, embarking on the North Atlantic "ferry" entailed only a week's exile at sea. In comparison, passage east from Tilbury to Bombay consumed three weeks while trips to Shanghai or Melbourne took a full month on board.

Consider too the climatic differential. Despite the year-round probability of gales or fog, transatlantic steamers traversed east/west bands of latitude, the weather en route more or less consistent. Passengers embarking in New York could disembark wearing the same wardrobe in Liverpool. But on vessels bound for the Far East, passengers who might be throwing snowballs on deck in the Channel would start wilting by Gibraltar and endure intolerable humidity in the Red Sea. Rather than visiting temperate New York, they were being engulfed within the tropics.

What about class distinctions? On board *Mauretania*, sailing between Liverpool and New York in 1907, the passenger load was accommodated either in the gilded comfort of First Class, the bourgeois respectability of Second, or, lowest on the socioeconomic ladder, the squalid discomfort in what was initially called Steerage, and, later, Third Class. But whatever the name of their purgatory, denizens of those lowest decks were light-years removed from their cosseted cabin shipmates inhabiting the upper decks.

On vessels steaming to the Far East, the class differential was blurred. Conditions in the Second Class were not that inferior to life in the First. The vast bulk of passengers, though not relocating for life, were bound east either on business or an assigned spell in the colonies. Returning to Blighty, the same passengers were heading home for leave, accompanied by colonial shipmates visiting the seat of empire.

One final differentiation distinguished Atlantic vessels from those destined for the East. Since the overwhelming majority of cabin clients were American, life on board was attuned to their tastes. Menus, clothing, music, and amusements reflected an unmistakable American slant. Indeed, the great transatlantic paradox was that those towering steamers, wrought in Scottish or Irish yards and flying Britain's merchant navy flag, offered a shipboard skewed towards the lucrative American market, Brit hegemony subtly revamped to please Yanks.

Peninsular & Oriental Steam Navigation Co.

The same standards prevailed on board French, Dutch, Italian, and German rivals as well. Aboard transatlantic vessels, regardless of national origin, America unquestionably ruled the waves.

But relatively few Americans booked cabins for India. Passage east was an all-British show. Passengers were almost exclusively British or British colonials eating British food within a totally British ethos. On board, they were looked after by the same turbaned, dark-skinned crewmen who would care for them under eastern skies. Most sailed east to administer an empire and sailed home having enjoyed the fruits of that empire. Indeed, the empire dictated all Far Eastern itineraries. For every tourist, planter, or grazier on board, there would be a dozen soldiers, bureaucrats, missionaries, or government functionaries, from High Commissioner to clerk.

So, for many Britons, the word steamer conjured up an image not of skyscrapers but a page from their geography primer—down a channel, across a bay, through straits, across a sea, through a canal, then another sea, and, finally, across several great oceans. And whereas during transatlantic passage nothing can be seen but cloud-banked horizon, passage east revealed an exotic continuum of ports—Gibraltar, Marseilles, Valetta, Port Said, Aden, Bombay, Colombo, Singapore, Hong Kong, Yokohama, Melbourne, and Sidney. In fact, the itinerary of necessity for steamships bound for the Far East evokes the almost standard litany of today's world cruise brochures.

Having established our Far Eastern context, it makes sense to divide our passages east into three separate categories. The first, for sailing ships only, around the tip of Africa to Australia; the second, for steamers, through the Straits of Gibraltar to Alexandria, and then overland to Suez and thence by sea to India; and, once de Lesseps's epic canal had been completed, aboard a new breed of larger, purpose-built steamers that conveyed passengers all the way from England to the Far East on the same vessel.

The wines are bad, some very bad, spirits very bad, soda water generally bad, ale and porter good. The officers attend well to their own comfort, particularly Purser Soden, but very little to that of the passengers.
—Unnamed P&O passenger, 1868

Passenger/diarist Smiles, a sixteen-year-old consumptive sailing to improve his health, boarded the fast sailing ship *Yorkshire* on February 20, 1869 for a 10,000-mile journey to Australia, three times the distance to New York. For many, it is a surprising fact of geographical life that passage around the Cape of Good Hope is only 550 miles longer than passage through the Mediterranean.

On the *Yorkshire*'s deck, as there would be for years aboard all Far Eastern passenger tonnage, were pens full of livestock as well as the ship's cow, which had been hauled up over the side by windlass and bellyband to be deposited within a stall forward by the galley.

For the First Class, *Yorkshire* boasted one large public room, a saloon that served as "our dining room, drawing room, and parlor, all in one." A long table had benches to either side with reversible backs and a single large chair for the master at its head. Along both walls of the saloon, insulating it from the sides of the vessel, were rows of cabins, their sliding doors latticed for ventilation—which would shortly prove essential—but as a result entailing total lack of privacy. Whatever transpired in every cabin became common knowledge; honeymooners, gossips, combatants, and snorers, beware.

Cabin bunks lined the inboard walls next to the saloon, made up with a plain white coverlet, a bookshelf, and swinging lamp suspended overhead. Along the far wall was a simple washstand, above which a gimbaled tray was provided for bottles. All manner of bagged necessities could be suspended from a row of hooks. Primitive bathrooms were down the corridor beyond the saloon.

There were only seventeen First Class passengers, all male save one, the Master's wife. An unspecified number traveled in the Second and Third Classes. Lunch was dished up at noon and dinner at 5:00 P.M. In between, reported Smiles, "we mooned about on deck," or read in the cabin.

Further south and into equatorial weather, the ship's bosun rigged a canvas tub on deck in which, early each morning, undressed passengers were drenched with a hose by a crewman. As the heat increased, young Smiles clambered aloft to cool off, although, on captain's orders, he was lashed to the rigging by solicitous crewmen.

Lassitude discouraged a dramatic committee although an amateur troupe of Christy's Minstrels did perform. Readings from Dickens were also organized. But without question, the greatest surge of excitement arose from encountering other vessels; sometimes three were sighted within the course of a single day. If one were homebound, *Yorkshire*'s captain would announce that a mail sack would

Malta, the ramparts of Valetta in 1860. The entrance to Grand Harbour is to the right, overlooked by the bastion containing the Lower Barracca Gardens. Note the emptiness of the streets in contrast to modern times.

The barren rocks of Aden. A photograph taken in the early days, probably before 1870, which gives a good impression of the desolate nature of the place.

be transferred so there was a lot of frantic letter writing as the two drew near. (One wonders what fresh bulletins could improve on heartfelt, pier-side farewells made only weeks earlier.) Typically, outbound *Yorkshire* delivered her letters while the inbound vessel—*Lord Raglan*—requested soap, newspapers, milk, and the services of *Yorkshire*'s surgeon. *Lord Raglan* was bound home from Bangkok to Yarmouth. Her master entertained his visitors with "Chinese beer and seegars" and dispatched a twenty-pound chest of tea back to the *Yorkshire*.

At the equator, the wind vanished, and canvas hung like a shroud. Within the span of the encircling horizon, diarist Smiles spotted no less than sixteen ships in the same predicament. But the wind returned, and, on the first day of April, passengers were roused early by an anonymous cry that a nearby ship was on fire. Everyone raced on deck only to find that the report was an ill-advised, but, as it turned out, prescient April Fool's joke.

Later that day, they spoke the German cargo vessel *Pyrmont*, also Yarmouth-bound, with a cargo of Chilean nitrate. She was carrying shipwrecked passengers from the burned-out *Blue Jacket*. The wretched survivors had been adrift in ship's boats for nine days before their rescue. *Yorkshire*'s passengers rallied 'round with welcome donations of clothing and shoes to the hapless castaways.

Deck sports cloying, amateur dramatics held sway and vignettes from *Pickwick Papers* were performed on the main hatch before a daytime audience of all three classes. Another sanctioned "sport"—complete with Baudelairian resonances—was slaughtering albatross. The poor creatures were caught, dispatched by the doctor with prussic acid, and then dismembered to provide grisly passenger souvenirs; one man fashioned a pipe stem out of a long wing bone, another created a tobacco pouch from the webbing of a foot.

More elaborate home brewed theatricals were mounted, *Sir Dagobart and the Dragon*, followed by *Aladdin and the Wonderful Scamp*. And as the vessel surged before prevailing westerlies towards Australia, the crew began cleaning and painting ship for arrival. A week before Melbourne landfall, the captain celebrated with a special dinner. It was an extraordinarily elaborate menu, given the distance from England and the primitive preservation standards of the day. Recorded Smiles: "There were ducks, fowls, tongues, hams with lobster salads, oyster pattes (sic), jellies, blanc-manges, and dessert." While passengers digested this spread, the saloon echoed with jests, songs, and toasts, and the festivities concluded with presentation of an elaborate testimonial to the master.

There are half a dozen gentlemen and four ladies only, the rest either cockney vulgarity or colonial impudence.

—F.R. Kendall

Yorkshire had remained at sea without touching land for 88 days. That marathon accumulation of consecutive sea days was possible only for vessels powered by canvas, a capability ironically curtailed by the arrival of steam. Whereas inexhaustible supplies of wind breezed over the taffrail, coal to fire boilers had to be stockpiled en route, and inordinate amounts were required to sustain steam passage east. In fact, P&O had to maintain three separate fleets before de Lesseps's canal made two of them redundant: one for passage east as far as Alexandria, another for continuing passage east beyond Suez, and a third to keep coal bunkers beyond Suez topped up. Though vessels of this last fleet were coal replenishers, they were driven, paradoxically, by canvas. Laden with Welsh anthracite, 170 chartered sailing colliers were regularly dispatched from Cardiff to rebunker the Mediterranean ports of Malta and Alexandria; for Far Eastern coaling ports such as Aden and Colombo, the colliers had to go 'round the Cape of Good Hope. For Suez coal stocks, as we shall see, the company employed a different method of delivery.

As of 1866, P&O routinely kept 20,900 tons of coal reserves in Aden, 10,000 tons in Hong Kong, and 12,000 tons at Point de Galle, south of Colombo. It cost the company over half a million pounds per annum to buy and deliver this vast stockpile. An overage was necessary, for tropical storage wreaked havoc with the coal's efficacy, reducing its thermal output by 20 percent.

In November of 1869, the same year that *Yorkshire* completed her three-month passage, Ferdinand de Lesseps opened his great Franco/Egyptian undertaking, the Suez Canal. Completion of the waterway would finally put paid to what had been euphemized in company prospectuses as "the overland route," an irksome but inevitable aspect of P&O's Far Eastern service. Pre-canal, in simplest terms, passengers bound for the East had to disembark from vessel A in Alexandria, proceed overland to Suez, and embark on vessel B to continue their voyage. Their two vessels differed in that the UK/Alexandria ships were crewed by Europeans, whereas those east of Suez boasted entirely Asian staff.

Consider the following typical P&O linked itineraries. *Massilia* sailed from Southampton on January 4, arriving at Gibraltar six days later. Passing through the Straits, she called at Malta on the 14th, before ending her voyage at Alexandria on the 19th. Meanwhile, scheduled at the same time, feeder steamer

The harbor at Bombay, 1870s.

Local craft at Penang, 1939.

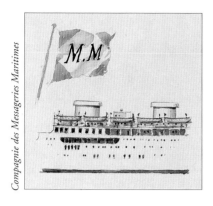

Compagnie des Messageries Maritimes

Nyanza would embark passengers and mail at Marseilles on France's Mediterranean coast, conclusion of yet another P&O overland alternative, about which more later. She would steam eastward, calling at Malta on the 14th before arriving at Alexandria on January 19, the same day as *Massilia*. Then, all passengers, their luggage, and the company mails from both vessels, would be sent overland to the northern end of the Red Sea to board waiting *Simla*. The day before, *Simla* had disembarked her passenger load bound for the mother country and was coaling for return to the subcontinent. With all of *Massilia's* and *Nyanza's* passengers and mails on board, she would set off south through the Red Sea on January 21, coal at Aden on the 26th, reach Colombo on February 4, to coal again before calling at Madras on February 7, and finally tie up in Calcutta on February 11.

Thirty-eight days had elapsed since original embarkation in Southampton. That obligatory, land-bound interruption imparted an almost surreal quality to the voyage. In mid-passage, passengers renounced the comforts of their ship and submitted to a taxing land journey before resuming sea life aboard a second vessel. A London luggage supplier—Allen's Portmanteaus—did a brisk trade in something called overland trunks, designed specifically to ease the logistical turmoil for travelers enduring this Egyptian stumbling block.

However tempting to conclude that this overland digression was unique, it was not: an identical disruption plagued travelers negotiating another isthmus, the one dividing Caribbean from Pacific at Panama. There, until completion of the canal in 1914, all passengers and freight aboard Pacific Mail Steamship Company vessels bound for America's west coast were off-loaded to cross the continental divide. At first, that overland interlude resembled the Egyptian one, a wet/dry parlay of canoe ferry up the Chagres River followed by a ghastly trek along festering jungle trails. But in 1850—a year after California's gold rush had begun—passengers crossed the isthmus to the Pacific aboard North America's first transcontinental railway train. Within three hours, they could embark aboard complementary Pacific Mail tonnage awaiting them at Panama City. The American euphemism was "the Isthmus over," a heaven-sent shortcut that saved travelers an additional 9,000-mile passage around the Horn.

Let us examine the ordeal of P&O's overland interlude. Shortly after sailing from Malta, a traditional ritual took place aboard eastbound P&O vessels, inevitable harbinger of the isthmus that lay over the horizon. Lots were drawn by all passengers, not to bet on the day's mileage or anchoring time, but to find out with whom one would share the six seats of a cramped, horse-drawn diligence. These vans, as they were called, would convey passengers along the last leg of their isthmus crossing, an eighty-five-mile desert track separating Cairo from Suez, before boarding their next ship. If one, or, worse, more than one, lady passenger were drawn for the same van, it was considered disadvantageous because their skirts occupied so much precious space.

But those vans were only the final of three separate modes of isthmus travel. As soon as the vessel moored at Alexandria after sunset, luggage and mails would come up from the hold and be swung ashore. At the same time, passengers would troop down gangways carrying the Victorian equivalent of hand luggage, and, thanks to warnings from the purser, supplies of bottled water and spirits. Before them lay a combined water and sand journey of 225 miles with a mid-point overnight at a Cairo hotel. Honoriah Lawrence recalls her Alexandrian landfall of 1848, a night without rest because "the mosquitoes were voracious, jackals howled and yelled; cocks began to crow about *sunset* (italics mine) and continued on and off till daylight."

First leg of the overland journey was by water, along a narrow canal linking Alexandria with the westernmost navigable tributary of the Nile delta. Eighteen feet deep but only nine feet wide at the bottom, the Mahmoudieh canal had been dug in 1819 under the direction of ruler Mehemet Ali with a huge workforce of 200,000 slaves. The forty-eight-mile ditch had been completed, one historian has claimed, in an astonishing five months.

The canal conveyance into which passengers embarked was called a track boat, a narrow barge drawn originally by horses and later by a steam tug called the *Afteh*, named after the village where the canal reached the Nile. (The little *Afteh* was, in fact, P&O's first iron vessel, prefabricated in England and shipped out to Egypt in pieces.) But whether drawn by horse or tug, track boats were unpleasantly crowded, filthy, and sometimes vermin-infested. Lady passengers berthed together in a communal cabin while their male fellow passengers dossed down wherever they could find room.

The contrast between this primitive barge and the relative luxe of the vessel they had just vacated was remarked by all. But there was nothing to be done; this was an inescapable hardship of passage east. Uncomfortably accommodated, passengers were hauled through the night, departing Alexandria at one in

Aden, Steamer Point in 1870. The black mounds are stocks of steam coal for bunkering. In the foreground is the local cab rank.

the morning to avoid some of the heat of the day. Sleep was rendered improbable by trumpet calls from a man stationed in the bow, trying to clear traffic ahead with prolonged blasts that were habitually ignored. Inevitably, there were frequent delays as their towing horses' reins had to be lifted over the masts of barges moored along the banks. At daybreak, those who wished to wash could only do so by drawing a bucketful of canal water up over the side.

At Afteh, passengers transferred to a river steamer—either the *Lotus* or the *Cairo*—much larger than the track boats but only slightly less cramped; below deck was a honeycomb of stifling cabins, or, for gentlemen, on-deck berthing that capitalized on whatever breezes were to be had. By that conveyance, passengers completed the journey's second leg, an overnight, 120-mile ascent of the Nile to Cairo where carriages delivered them either to Shepheard's or the French-owned Hotel d'Orient, or P&O's own transit hotel.

Cairo was P&O's passenger watershed, for it was there, in the lobbies, corridors, and dining rooms of those newly-established caravanseries that eastbound and returning westbound voyagers would meet, at the apogee of their two respective journeys. They had plenty to talk about. However fabled their latter-day reputation, mid-19th century conditions within those grand Cairo hotels were not always salubrious. One jaundiced traveler compiled a list of hotel pests that included "mosquitoes, bugs, fleas, midges, sand flies, and the like."

The next morning was what, in modern touring parlance, would be called a free day. Males inevitably flocked to local haberdashers and emerged self-consciously wearing solar topees. Then they hired donkeys and their rascally handlers for a seven-mile trip to gape at, or, in some instances, clamber up the pyramids. An outing restricted to male passengers only was a visit to Cairo's slave market. But whatever the passengers' tastes, the sights, smells, and sounds of Cairo proved hypnotic. This was, for every newcomer, first heady embrace of the Eastern experience, an East seen not from the elusive aerie of a ship's railing but in the roiling midst of mosque, marketplace, and souk. One traveler encapsulated the flavor of the Egyptian capital's streets, thronged with "green turbaned sherifs, blue-turbaned copts, red-fezzed frock-coated officials, and extremely naked children..."

While these intrepid P&O travelers rest up for the next stage of their overland journey, we must return momentarily to Alexandria to document the

Aden, with a British India steamer coaling offshore.

British India Steam Navigation Company, Ltd.

extraordinary means by which their hold baggage, as well as hundreds of mail sacks, would cross the desert to join them at Suez. Vast camel trains, thousands strong, were assembled at the Alexandrian docks. Each beast was loaded, one after the other, until the ship's holds had been emptied. (About 3,500 camels, it was reckoned, were required for the contents of a 3,000-ton steamer.)

Long before embarkation back in England, passengers had been issued stringent instructions about the maximum size of trunks or valises: on no account could they exceed either eighty pounds in weight or greater volume than 2'3" x 1'2" x 1'2". This had nothing to do with cabin or hold limitations, but the maximum weight and/or dimension that could be slung to either side of a camel's saddle for the slog to Suez. Each beast carried no more than 160 pounds of something, either luggage, mails, or sometimes, sacks of coal. Since the company's sailing colliers could not penetrate the windless northern reaches of the Red Sea, Suez's bunkers had to be replenished overland. Thousands of tons of coal, off-loaded in Alexandria, were routinely humped by camel train across the desert to Suez.

Checking out of their Cairo hotels, passengers made their first acquaintance with the notorious vans. These were wooden conveyances, approximately the size of seaside bathing machines familiar from Brighton. Inside, two benches faced inward along either side and a semicircular canvas cover—the tilt, it was called—protected occupants from sun, dust, wind, or at night, cold. Each van carried six occupants en face, knees interlocked; all but the shortest had to keep their heads awkwardly bent to avoid the encroaching tilt. Similar to the early Roman chariot called a quadriga—two-wheeled and drawn by four horses—the vans were devoid of springs, offering a ride more farm cart than fiacre. The eighty-five miles to Suez would be achieved in excruciating stages along a road, so-called, the surface of which deteriorated the further it meandered from Cairo. Shipboard classes traveled in segregated vans, although there was scant difference between First and Second Class interiors; all were universally uncomfortable.

The number "four" seems to have governed van logistics. Drawn by teams of four horses (or two mules and two horses), convoys of four vans were dispatched from Cairo or Suez at strict, four-hour intervals, presumably to facilitate the rota of resting horses that would suit traffic in both directions. Horses and/or mules were routinely changed every eight miles; one can only assume either that the poor beasts were maltreated and overworked, or, that surface conditions were so appalling that eight miles did them in.

While the animals were changed, passengers descended to stretch their legs and avail themselves of refreshments at a rest house, a chain of which stretched all the way to Suez. The most elaborate was—quadripartite yet again—number four, a halfway house larger than the others and equipped with a water tower, stables, and rooms for not only ladies and gentlemen, but their servants as well. The water tower was not sited over a well but had to be filled by horse-drawn tanker deliveries of Nile water filtered through earthenware jars.

All rest house dining rooms offered meals that, on paper, sound presentable: chickens, pigeon, mutton, and fruit adorned the bill of fare. But sanitary conditions were problematic. Wrote one fastidious lady passenger new to the Middle East: "The tables, wall, ceiling, and floor were literally swarming with flies. When I lay down on a divan, I was covered from head to foot. Breakfast dishes were indescribable because they were also covered with flies and they entered our mouths when trying to eat." Egyptian house flies, smaller than those familiar to Britons, were persistent, aggravating, and without numbers. There were also fleas, which, though kept down on the Nile boats by diligent applications of chloride of lime, flourished in every desert rest house. But Honoriah Lawrence recalls a kind of alfresco charm about her rest house breakfast at dawn: "A table prepared in the wilderness; cold fowl, hash, potatoes, tea, and coffee; just our little group of life in the midst of that wild waste."

As on the track boats, most of the travel took place overnight to spare both animals and passengers from the desert sun. But the jolting of the vans was so hideously pronounced that no one slept. One young man called Thomas Sutherland—later a P&O chairman—recorded his impressions of an 1856 overland trek:

"The road was merely a cutting in the sand which in the nighttime was not distinguishable from the desert itself. Indeed, it was a very frequent occurrence for the horses to stray into the desert when the driver supposed he was in the middle of the road...A moonlight journey was most striking. The seemingly boundless expanse, the silence only broken by the voice of the driver, and the muffled sound of horse's feet...the caravans loaded with mails and baggage passing with silent and stealthy tread, the whitened bones of countless troops of camels which had died in harness, glistening in the moonlight..."

The silence that Sutherland remembered suggests that small talk among his fellow occupants had long since been exhausted. Yet despite the heat, jolting misery, plagues of insects, and inedible fare, that trans-Egyptian journey—by track boat, steamer, and van—recalls the somehow evocative hardship of the Victorian abroad, adventure of a kind rarely encountered today, and certainly never inflicted on contemporary passengers. Tourist busses and Hilton hotels have long since conquered that desert and demanding detours like the overland route are no more. For the neophyte voyager, it may have been a testing novelty but for the repeat traveler, a numbing replay.

Another route led to the Red Sea port of Qusier, 250 miles south of Suez. This was offered for the convenience of passengers, who, eschewing Cairo, remained aboard the Nile boats as far upriver as Luxor. Having marveled at the temples, these sightseers then boarded a similar shuttle of vans to negotiate a similarly abysmal track to their vessel awaiting them in the Red Sea. In 1858, long overdue, a railway was completed across the desert to Suez. Impeccably clean and luxurious to start, within five years conditions aboard that British-built rolling stock had deteriorated so badly that by the time the canal was completed

a decade later, the carriages were as verminous and primitive as the rest house chain they had supplanted. Read the Orient Guide of 1888: "The train is very slow, and the carriages by no means too comfortable, with windows that let in the dust and doors which will neither shut tight nor open easily."

Final postscript to that unlamented Egyptian interlude, travelers reunited with their luggage at Suez were appalled at the damage that had been sustained en route. One unhappy man whose "overland trunk" proved pervious to the rigors of camel travel found that two bottles—one of hair oil and another of ink—had broken, sullying much of his brand-new, Far Eastern kit.

All was hurry and confusion on board, passengers crying and lamenting on leaving their friends and relations, some hunting their luggage without effect, pigs grunting, calves bellowing, cocks crowing, geese screaming, crew drunk, officers swearing, steam blowing off, other passengers seeking after their berths— in short, a thousand like this, which made all confusion and riot.

—Passenger description of a P&O sailing from Hythe

Sydney, SS Northam *entering Port Jackson, 1862.*
The ship was an iron screw steamer of 1330 g.r.t. built to fulfill the mail contract to Australia which was awarded to P & O in 1852. Her builders were Summers, Day & Co of Northam, near Southampton.
The approaches to Sydney Harbour were fortified against possible Russian attack at the time of the Crimean War.

Passengers on the RMS Arcadia, *1894.*

A Nile houseboat with lateen rig.

Even after Ferdinand de Lesseps had successfully breached the isthmus, the British regarded his achievement with combined reluctance and ill-feeling. They had long derided the proposed canal as impossible. Was it impossible, or, more likely, impertinent? Lord Palmerston was not alone in suspecting that "the proposal was merely a device for French interference in the east." Having thwarted Bonaparte's Middle Eastern aggrandizement at the Battle of the Nile, Britons did not take kindly to a resurgence of Franco-Egyptian connivance. One of Parliament's most qualified scientific members, Robert Stephenson, the engineer who had perfected locomotives and built wondrous bridges, expounded at length to his fellow MP's on the unfeasibility of a canal at Suez; he died ten years before its successful completion.

Canal bashing was not confined to Whitehall; even P&O had, to employ a gritty desert synonym, kept their heads firmly in the sand. In the late 1860s, at the same time as de Lesseps's mechanical diggers were displacing thousands of tons of spoil, the company had invested heavily in new tonnage, buttressing their traditional, two-fleet sinews. A flotilla of newbuilding destined for P&O plunged into the waters around Great Britain: in 1865, *Tanjore*, *Mongolia*, and *Niphon*; the following year, *Geelong*, *Malacca*, *Avoca*, *Sunda*, and *Surat*; and in 1867, *Bangalore*, *Sumatra*, and *Travancore* entered service. All were engined with two-cylinder, direct-action horizontal engines, and none displaced more than 3,000 tons. The largest of this pre-canal fleet was *Mongolia*, designed for service between Suez and Calcutta.

There are some indications that de Lesseps, plagued with cost overruns, may have opened his canal too soon. There were sections along its ninety-nine-mile length that on opening day in November of 1869 still gave trouble. Hinted one British journalist: "There are captious people who say the canal they came to see does not exist."

It was only on September 10, 1869, that Mediterranean water had first been admitted into the centrally located Bitter Lakes. (Picture the canal as roughly a straight line piercing two existing bodies of water, Timsah and Bitter Lakes.) Ten days later, de Lesseps and his chief engineer, Monsieur Voisin, had achieved the first complete passage from Port Said through to Suez without incident, a journey that consumed only fifteen hours. However, they were traveling in a small tug called *Latiff*.

Preparatory to the grand opening less than two months later, British warships *Prince Consort* and *Royal Oak* ran aground in the approaches to Port Said, temporarily stuck in the mud of a giant spoil bank. As the parade of

Orient Steam Navigation Company, Ltd.

vessels, including France's royal yacht *L'Aigle* with Empress Eugénie on board, steamed cautiously south along the canal, several ran aground; even the little *Latiff* was immobilized for two days. Among that festive flotilla was the little P&O paddle-wheeler *Delta*, carrying a delegation of company directors and a commander on the bridge worried sick about grounding; the P&O vessel probed only as far south as Lake Timsah before turning back.

However lavish the Viceroy's opening festivities, the maritime response was cautionary. In the vicinity of one obstruction, La Serapeum Rock, water was rumored to be no more than eighteen and a half feet deep, well short of the canal's officially promulgated working depth of twenty-two feet. Crossing Lake Timsah—perhaps that was what worried *Delta*'s commander—the channel seemed very much a work in progress, marked by wooden posts topped with red and white crosses. But, ready or not, perhaps the special correspondent for the *London Times* summed it up best: "Everyone accepts the canal as an accomplished work. It may be deepened or widened or both but the canal is made."

That historic waterway would change P&O's world dramatically—their schedules, their mail service, and, most critically, their newbuilding philosophy. Tonnage had to be amplified into a single fleet of larger ships that would be crewed, provisioned, and maintained entirely from Britain. Just as the dimensions of today's cruise ships are restricted by the 1,000' x 110' dimensions of Panama's locks, so P&O and Orient Line tonnage in the last century were built to the limitations of the canal at Suez. It was initially quite narrow, which meant that passing boats meeting in the straightaway sometimes had to yield, mooring in lay-bys cut into the banks. Later on, the canal would be widened and also electrified so that it could function through the night. Earliest transits of forty-eight hours were gradually reduced to twenty-four.

Whatever doubts about the efficacy of the Suez Canal before construction, incremental tonnage figures to follow (most of it British) offered ample justification. During its first full year of operation in 1870, slightly less than half a million tons of shipping passed through it. By 1898, the annual figure had increased to over nine million tons.

Maritime focus in the eastern Mediterranean shifted from Alexandria to Port Said, newly created destination that served as the canal's northern terminus;

de Lesseps had named it after Said Pasha, Viceroy of Egypt. Two-ship voyages for passage east were over and the "east via the overland route" was replaced by "through working" vessels. But if the intolerable desert vans could be junked, overland trains remained a ludicrous fact of P&O life for several more years, due to the pompous officialdom of the Royal Mail. P&O's contract with Her Majesty's government specified that the mails to or from the East were to be conveyed "overland via Suez." So despite the newly-wrought waterway, for several years, British mail sacks were solemnly disembarked at Suez, loaded aboard railway vans to cross the desert for reembarkation at Alexandria. Meanwhile, the ship and all her passengers had slipped effortlessly through the canal.

While on the subject of the mails, it is worth a small detour to consider their supreme importance in the financial health of passage east. It would be safe to say that no long-range sustainable passenger service, from Britain to the east, or south to Africa, or west to America, could survive without the economic underpinning of a mail contract; P&O's annual subsidy in 1840 was a lucrative £150,000.

Responsibility for carrying the mails was a serious business. Initially, embarkation and distribution of the precious sacks were considered the responsibility of the Admiralty. Each ship's mail officer was a member of the Royal Navy, given enormous powers of discretion and able to override the master, or, as he was traditionally called on P&O tonnage, the commander. On more than one occasion, once eastbound mail had been retrieved from the camel train and embarked at Suez, the mail officer would order his vessel to sea, even though passenger vans were still toiling across the desert. This arrogant government prerogative was finally relinquished in 1871; once Royal Naval functionaries had disembarked forever, P&O third officers took over in their place and commanders retained their customary shipboard autonomy.

To speed their eastern mail delivery time, the company decided to load mails on board their ships at Marseilles rather than Tilbury or Southampton. An entire week could be saved by this overland stratagem. Everyday, a train composed entirely of mail vans would leave London's Cannon Street Station bound for the south of France. Each mail sack bore a color-coded tag to alleviate the mail officer's chore when off-loading: gray indicated bags for Port Said and the Middle East, pink for Aden and East Africa, buff for Bombay, and red and white for Ceylon. The port of destination was also painted prominently on every sack.

Thus encoded, eastern mail would cross the Channel to Calais and rattle south across France. Forward of the mail vans were passenger carriages, provided for two types of Far Eastern traveler: Either the dilatory who wished to avail themselves of an additional week in the United Kingdom, or, more numerous, the squeamish avoiding the Bay of Biscay. The train was a crack express, its *chef du train* an impressive individual called Napoleon.

Snaking through the Marseilles docks, the mail train would arrive alongside P&O's pier. While passengers and their luggage transferred from train to vessel, mail sacks were unloaded and stacked along the concrete wharf opposite the appropriate hatches: forward Bombay and Colombo, number two hatch Australia etc. Once the accumulating mountains of mail sacks had been counted, checked, and rechecked, each was carried up the sloping gangway by a Marseilles stevedore past the Mail Officer, lantern in hand, who tallied each one into his record book as it passed. Embarking the mails might last throughout the night and only when the process had been completed to the mail officer's entire satisfaction was the commander permitted to sail.

After the outbreak of the Franco-Prussian war in 1870, P&O extended their overland linkage to the port of Brindisi, just above the heel of Italy's boot. Now the Cannon Street mail vans and the passenger rolling stock faced a longer continental run, in effect, an interminable boat-train approach that consumed an entire weekend. First Class passengers paid sixteen pounds, eighteen shillings each, including both rail ticket and a sleeping berth supplement.

Though ostensibly established as a wartime expedient, the Brindisi express long outlasted hostilities. In 1891, for example, the train puffed out of Victoria or Charing Cross each Friday afternoon for Folkestone. After landing at Calais, the train continued through Paris and south to Lyon before bearing east and crossing into Italy at Modane. There, at four in the morning, passengers had to submit to a customs inspection before boarding their Italian train. They carried with them carpetbags and rugs from their sleeping compartment; larger items of baggage (and they were larger, for the 80-1b camel limitation had long since been abrogated) were manhandled by an army of porters from the French vans, through the customs shed and into the Italian vans. The express finally puffed into Brindisi's ocean terminal at 4 P.M. on Sunday, forty-eight hours after London departure.

Nederland Stoomvaart Maatschappij

Though the mails arrived to the company's satisfaction, passenger satisfaction aboard the Brindisi express proved elusive.

Port Said, looking south from the top of the lighthouse tower with the entrance to the canal in the background, late 1880s. The ship in the foreground is a French ironclad, either Vauban *or her sister ship* Duguesclin. *Completed in 1885, these ships mounted four 9.4-inch guns in twin barbettes, one on each beam, and were protected by a belt of 6-inch to 10-inch thick wrought iron armor.*

Hong Kong, view of the waterfront with the head office of the Hong Kong-
Shanghai Bank on the left, overlooked by Government House on the hill behind.
The Peak Tram railway appears to be under construction; this was opened in
1888.

Brocklebank, Thomas & Jonathan, Ltd.

Travelers complained about the uneven roadbed, slovenly staff, indifferent food, and, in winter, the cold, only partially alleviated by large foot warmers installed in every compartment. One Major General on his way home from India wrote P&O describing the "chaos at Brindisi;" merely getting from steamer to train he found confusing. Once on the train, he felt obliged to give up his (prepaid) berth to a female shipmate while he slept on the floor of the dining car, in which the food, he reported, was "dear and not good." Washing arrangements were inadequate, and the constant, jiggling rattle of fittings and glass lamps intolerable. Finally, the general's dispatch box and portmanteau, carefully labeled, had been thrown into the luggage van and damaged. There was "much comment," he concluded darkly, "about the Brindisi express all over India."

The Orient Line offered the same overland service to Naples with, predictably, the same grudging passenger response. In truth, the bleak probability was that a Victorian transcontinental train journey of 1,459 miles, regardless how obsequious the staff or diligent the chef, proved as irritating as it was exhausting, predestined to end in rumpled distress. Even a P&O guidebook of the period acknowledged that train ride to be "a somewhat tedious and expensive journey." Some passengers broke their journey in Paris or Turin, thus reducing the duration and extent of their railway compartment fever.

The heaviest mail flow was outbound, towards the East. And as the numbers of mail bags proliferated, the dimension of P&O's below-deck post offices had often to be augmented. One internal report suggested that conditions were so inadequate that shipboard postal clerks had to sort the mail on deck, atop the after hatch, and that curious passengers, on the lookout for letters to themselves, would rummage through it. So two cabins adjacent to the postal office were appropriated, eighty additional square feet that translated into a third more space.

But regardless, passengers still badgered the postal clerks: "We have asked the Mail Agent on board to hunt thro' the letters as he sorts them and give us any there may be for us..." wrote a Scotswoman, Lizzie Bradford, to a friend at home. An intrepid traveler to the Far East, she was the wife of Edward Bradford, who served in India as agent to the Governor General of Rajputana.

The words of this articulate passenger will recur in the pages to follow, kindness of her great-grandson Andrew Bradford of Kincardine.

Swinging cot, hair mattress, feather pillow, ship couch or sofa, case of blacking, brushes, footbath and tin can for water; 48 longcloth shirts, 24 longcloth full-front nightshirts, 24 Indian gauze waistcoats, 128 nightcaps, 72 cotton half-hose, 12 silk ditto and 12 woolen ditto.

—Recommended kit for Far Eastern travelers, 1850

Let us share a passage east just before the turn of the century. Long before embarkation, travelers shopped all over London to equip themselves for the rigors ahead, the equivalent for neophytes of a voyage into the unknown. But there was no shortage of accomplished purveyors to advise them. As a result, packed within their carpet bags, portmanteaus, holdalls, dress baskets, and cabin trunks, was a variety of arcane haberdashery. Some men bought patented "sans-plis" shirts: "Being entirely free from gathers, it is cooler, much stronger, and will bear the Indian mode of washing better than any shirt in use," advised the manufacturer. The house of Sampson & Co., Shirt Tailors and Outfitters, advertised a "complete India outfit" for the astonishing figure of only £38. Included in the outfit were a dozen linen front white shirts, four suits—two brown linen, one blue serge, and one tropical flannel—six sleeping pajama suits, a laundry bag complete with frame and lock, a sun umbrella, an anti-cholera belt, pith helmet, and two pairs of "unvulcanized" suspenders.

Far Eastern kit requirements extended well into the 20th century. In 1926, William MacQuitty was advised by the bank employing him in India that he would "require one cabin trunk, one large tin-lined wood chest, and two suitcases. Besides ordinary clothes, you will require evening dress, a dozen stiff white shirts, two dozen collars ditto, a dozen white shirts, mosquito boots, and two tropical suits. The Indian tailor will copy as many more as you may require very cheaply. You will purchase your solar topee at Simon Artz in Port Said."

Together with solar topees, cholera belts, mosquito boots, and dozens of nightcaps, additional equipment was required for passage east near the end of the century. Goy, Limited, of Leadenhall Street ("Outfits to All Parts of the World and to All Classes" and just down the street from P&O headquarters) advertised itself as the "Passengers' and Emigrants' Outfitter." The company offered a full

RANGOON RIVER, THE MOULMEIN STEAMER ARRIVING

Rangoon River, the Moulmein steamer arriving, 1903. SS Rangoon, *British India Line,*
built in 1875.

Burmese prahu, *or war canoe, on the Irrawaddy, 1870.*

Nice, in the South of France. The late nineteenth century photograph gives an impression of the Mediterranean coast and of the local craft which would have been familiar also in the nearby ports of Marseilles and Genoa.

Venice, with what appears to be an Italian naval paddle dispatch vessel in the foreground. In the background is the church of San Giorgio Maggiore at the eastern extremity of the island of La Giudecca. The date is about 1870.

Mount Lavinia Hotel, near Colombo, Ceylon.

line of chairs for steamers, including deck seats, cane chairs with arms, three types of cane lounges (plain, reclining, and with folding backs that held five positions), and folding hammock chairs. There was a wide variety of cabin trunks, some made up in leather but others, with a prescient eye on Far Eastern humidity, "airtight tin trunks."

Passengers boarded their ship in Tilbury at the mouth of the Thames. Southampton embarkations were no more. All the mails went by train to Brindisi and shippers of freight refused to pay supplementary land haulage to England's south coast. For passengers fearful of sea motion, Southampton sailings avoided a full day's Channel steaming. By the same token, those faint-of-heart could also travel on the mail train to Brindisi but would still suffer a Channel crossing on the rail ferry. For our purposes, I think it makes sense that we document the entire passage east by sea.

After a complimentary train ride down river from London, passengers embarked via a very steep gangway. What made it steep was that no opening in the promenade deck bulkhead had been provided to accommodate it. So passengers had to climb over the top of the ship's rail, then onto a four-step unit that brought them down to deck level. Lascar seamen clad in their UK, cold-weather rig of blue serge, helped passengers descend.

They repaired at once to their assigned cabins, following the route indicated by cardboard notices pinned to alleyway walls. This was inevitably a moment of keenest angst, not only to absorb the dimensions of the chamber that would serve as their home for the voyage, but, for single travelers, encountering those with whom that home must be shared. Cabin size was modest. Some years earlier, novelist William Makepiece Thackeray had lamented about being "doubled, trebled, or quadrupled with perfect strangers for three weeks in a space the size of a four-poster bed."

By the nineties, cabin tenancy to Bombay had been reduced to three weeks, but, in crowded or uncongenial proximity, three weeks might seem an eternity. Differing standards of hygiene provoked discord. One occupant of a multi-berthed shipboard domicile did not endear himself to cabinmates by wearing the same brown woolen trousers from Tilbury to Bombay. "You can always get along with a fellow," suggested one missionary feelingly, "who is punctually loyal to King Tub."

Unlike our friend Smiles's cabin on the sailing vessel years earlier, there was almost no shelving or furniture, only a washstand and camp stool. Cabin trunks—never more than fourteen inches high—jockeyed for space beneath lower bunks. One advantage over Smiles's cabin was that there was electric light, not at the head of each berth, but a single ceiling fixture with the switch by the door. Dressing for dinner, it would turn out, had to be done in shifts by mutual agreement. There were, by the mid-1890s, bathrooms between cabins, but they were, according to ship's regulations, not used in the Red Sea, because, in delicate company parlance, they did not "remain sweet."

Second Class cabins were even more crowded. "Six passengers," recorded one occupant, "inside a cabin fit only for two. With these temporary berths, I could not turn over without moving other passengers and we had to wait to shave and dress. It was not," he concluded, "as pretty as the brochure." Lizzie Bradford had her own vision of Second Class: "And I couldn't bear that Baby should sleep in the stuffy, 2nd class part of the ship, which is quite at the other end, and the only way to get at it is along the deck, thro' all the kitchen, and coaling and animals and about 10 people in a cabin when you get there."

On board Orient Line vessels, only one parcel was allowed per passenger in the cabin, its dimensions 2'8" long, 1'6" wide, and 1'2" high, only slightly larger than P&O's camel restrictions from the overland days. All the rest, suitably tagged either WANTED ON VOYAGE or NOT WANTED ON VOYAGE, was consigned to the care of the Fourth Officer who saw to its disposition below in the baggage room. There, the WANTED ON VOYAGE luggage would be available to passengers on a weekly basis as the weather changed. Descent to the heaving, stifling confusion of the baggage room in search of replacement clothing was a symptomatic ordeal for wives as their vessel ploughed relentlessly eastward.

The Fourth Officer was not immune from error. Lizzie Bradford wrote to her father aboard an unnamed P&O vessel: "Another time, I will not employ an agent to put one's things aboard for they merely did exactly that and nothing more and everything was stuck down into the hold at once—even the chair and the box labeled 'Cabin' and which was all I wanted for the first fortnight of the voyage. I sent for the Purser and he referred me to some other officer who I hunted up and all he said was that everything was down in the hold and could not now be got up till next Friday the 25th! So till then we haven't a thing but the clothes we came on board in and Baby has no nightgown and has to wear one of mine which I luckily stuffed into the carpet bag the last morning..."

Harrison, T. & J.

Shipping in the Hooghly, Calcutta, 1865

Little folding carpet stools were ubiquitous on board; originally brought from home, now they were provided by the company for use not only in the cabin—their lightness and collapsibility an advantage—but also out on deck. Since they were common ship's furniture, identical carpet stools tended to migrate all over the vessel. Sometimes, oily ones used by engineers below inadvertently found their way to passenger country, soiling ladies' dresses. To avoid this, engineer stools always had one leg painted white, which lady passengers learned to avoid. However, individual deck chairs were still carried aboard by passengers, to be committed to the depths of a noisome, on-deck locker, ready for daily retrieval when weather permitted. One firm stipulation about all passengers' deck chairs was that they be identified with the owners' name on the front, not the back; otherwise, entire rows of seated passengers might be discommoded by dogged shipmates on the trail of a purloined chair. And regardless of what Goy, Limited was promoting back in London, "folding hammock chairs" were no good afloat because their canvas seats retained ocean damp.

Luggage deposited, and, where appropriate, cabinmates appraised, passengers ventured forth to explore the vessel. After sleep, food was most important and the dining saloon was inevitably the next destination after the cabin. Passengers found rows of tables lined with cast-iron swivel chairs bolted to the deck. The ship's mast plunged down through the central table and removable fiddles providing compartmental security against sea motion for plates, mugs, and glasses. Overhead, there were racks for condiments and glasses. Above the racks was suspended a stiffened, horizontal length of brocade which confused first-time passengers; it was, of course, the breeze-making Indian punka, which, unused at Tilbury, would become indispensible in the Red Sea.

By the end of the century, catering standards had been immeasurably improved by the provision, in 1879, of shipboard refrigeration. Orient Line's

Bibby Brothers & Company

Orient was the first electrified vessel sailing to the East; others quickly followed suit. Prior to then, P&O had bought 1,360 tons of Canadian ice annually, which arrived in Bombay packed in sawdust. (David McCullough, in *The Path Between the Seas*, documents the economics of shepherding ice through the tropics. Of 700 tons loaded in Boston, 600 arrived in Panama City; another 400 tons melted getting it ashore but the profit on the 200-ton balance more than offset all losses.)

With the installation of ice-making equipment, a refrigeration mechanic was added to the crew manifest, and notorious, on-deck menageries could be dispensed with, as could their keepers and bushels of feed. P&O's annual purchase of livestock had been substantial: 592 oxen, 69 calves, 13,105 sheep, 3,504 pigs, and 160,163 poultry. The noise and stink of what was essentially a floating farmyard had long been a perennial feature of Far Eastern travel. P&O set up a huge ice-making plant at Suez, and, at Tilbury, meat arrived aboard on hooks rather than on the hoof. A ready supply of ice was a boon for passengers traveling through a hot climate although it should be noted that P&O was extremely chary about how much ice should be dispensed to the passengers. Sniffed one company inspector after an "industrial espionage" crossing on the American Line's *St. Louis* in 1904: "Ice wastefully used at meals and all other times."

Mention of ice, of course, leads irresistibly to the subject of strong drink. One of the most remarkable aspects of P&O perquisites until 1874 was that onboard, drink was free, part—and for some, a very substantial part—of normal passage fare. Spirits, wines, and beer were provided gratis by the company to the tune of 1,301,608 aggregate of bottles each year, including whiskey, brandy, gin, rum, and, overall winner at more than half a million bottles, pale ale. The company also bottled an extremely good claret, a practice that Lord Jeffrey Sterling, present P&O chairman, is in the process of reviving.

Although free, drink was not dispensed that liberally. A Purser's Standing Order circa 1860 read "Do not overload the tables with either eatables or drinkables." But free drinkables went by the board in 1874 and it is interesting to note how Purser's Standing Orders had been adjusted by 1888: "It is not the first object of your work to keep down expenditure, but it is your first duty to see a table of superior quality maintained on board your ship, and your passengers thoroughly well satisfied. It has seldom happened that a really good table was not an economical one..."

Of course, charging passengers for drinks opened a Pandora's box of dishonesty and bilking. In 1901, an unscrupulous barman aboard *Australia* ran an extremely profitable scam when dispensing whiskey. A full glass cost sixpence; when passengers requested a half glass, the barman would plead that he had no change and keep the entire sixpence. Each transaction meant thruppence for him until a company inspector, traveling incognito, put a stop to it.

Under way down the broad Thames estuary, the Gravesend pilot was dropped and the vessel headed towards—but clear of— the Goodwin Sands preparatory to rounding the southeastern tip of Britain. Once more or less settled-in and tucking into their first lunch, passengers' great preoccupation—aboard every ship going everywhere—was surreptitious evaluation of their fellows. Most sharing passage east were compatible. A very typical passenger cross-section from the mid-1890's was "officers, civil servants, wives, and families going out for the cold season, Members of Parliament visiting India, businessmen going out to sell wares, youths looking for fame or fortune, and fair maidens going out to be married."

Those young ladies not affianced but on the lookout were known throughout the Far East as "the fishing fleet." Aboard *Malma* in 1874, Lizzie Bradford wrote: "We have two or three young ladies on board and we amuse ourselves with watching who they walk about with, and sit with after dark—and all sorts of funny things go on—or we hear they do." Even married ladies could be a problem. "There is a horrid Mrs. Wilkes, rather young and hideous I think, going out to her husband, who behaves abominably. She sits up till past 12, with one or two young officers, and gets one of the girls to do it too, if she can, and the other night they were all found drinking brandy and soda in the doctor's cabin at midnight. Queer creatures."

Victorian reticence about the subject was such that little has been recorded about sexual dalliance on board vessels bound for the East. Some self-appointed chaperones kept it to a minimum. Aboard *Oriental*, it was written that "there was only one Miss Pruneprism—a man—who kept an eye if two canvas chairs were too close together under the shade of the boats by moonlight. But there were no bounders or cads..."

Or were there? Another observer outlined what was apparently a fairly common scenario: "Strange tales have been told, and vouched for, of young

Alfred Holt & Company

ladies taking with them their trousseau, ready for the prearranged meeting with the expectant bridegroom at the port of destination, changing their minds en route, and landing at an intermediate port to share their lot with a newly-found cavalier, whose acquaintance was perhaps only begun on the Mediterranean." History does not record how many no-

show fiancées there were; however, it is certain that everyone on board was privy to each ruinous lapse. Small wonder that every passage east, it was said, ended with at least one engagement and one duel.

Once down Channel, outbound vessels approached Ushant, France's northwestern corner, passing which would herald entry into the dread waters of the Bay of Biscay. This was passage east's most notoriously rough leg, all the more so since for outbound vessels, it came at the start of the voyage, well before passengers had acquired any semblance of sea legs. There were some passengers on early vessels who preferred to sit up throughout those rough nights. Compounding the Biscayan ordeal, if the seas were menacing, it might take seventy-two as opposed to thirty-six hours for the crossing. Inside sickroom/cabins, toppled carpet stools and upturned luggage littered the floor, green water thundered against the ship's side, and whatever nourishment the steward brought lay untouched and congealing. Children well enough to sit at the dining table were taped securely into their swivel chairs. It was Thackeray who knew that Portugal was on the horizon only because the groans of the sick no longer emanated from cabin rows lining the saloon.

Past Lisbon, the stop at Gibraltar was a short one since there was no coal depot and certainly no water; at two shillings-and-thruppence per hundred gallons, marine superintendents considered it criminally overpriced. (In fact, water on the Rock has always been perennially scarce, collected from sloping rainwater catchments on its eastern side.) There were fruit and cigars to buy from a flock of bumboats besieging the companionway but time for no more than brief excursions ashore to peer at the fortifications.

It has been said by some unappreciative person that only six occupations can be indulged by those who travel by sea, viz.: to eat, drink, sleep, flirt, quarrel, or grumble. To those a seventh may well be added—to smoke; and of all seven we get, perhaps, more than a normal share on a fine day in the tropics.
—P&O Guide Book, 1888

Once through the Straits and into the Mediterranean, outdoors ruled shipboard life. Although Mediterranean storms could blow up suddenly and precipitously, by and large "the clerk of the weather was kind," and most passengers who had found their sea legs unearthed chairs from the locker and staked out their own favorite sections of the upper promenade, or, as it was called, the hurricane deck.

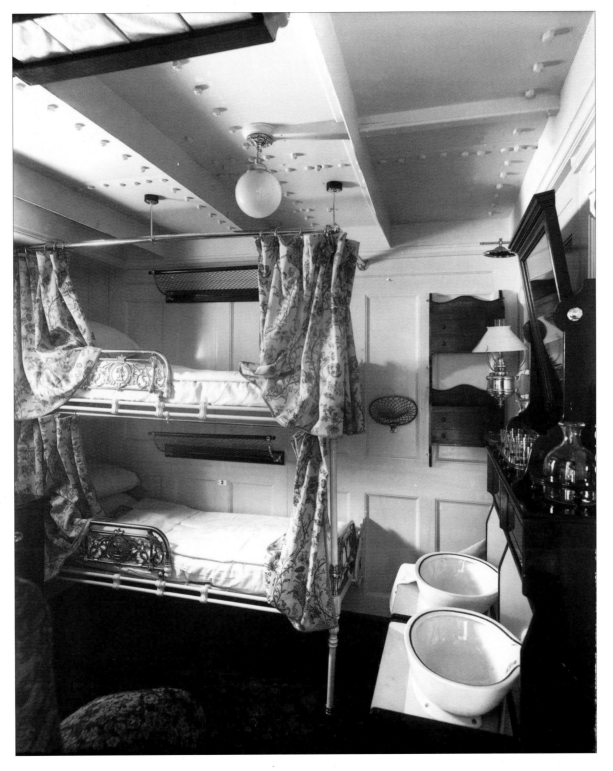

Two-berth cabin in the Cunarder Saxonia, *1900.*

Singapore, Victoria Dock.

It was symptomatic of passage east that hour after hour was passed on deck. Past Suez, as we shall see, that on-deck tenancy might well last the night. It was this fact of shipboard life that dictated the vessels' general arrangement; interior public rooms and cabins were far more modest than on North Atlantic tonnage quite simply because so much less time was spent indoors. And although there were no conventional promenade or shelter decks, there was shelter of another kind: awnings covered most open decks east of Gibraltar. In the Mediterranean, they were dismantled each night; but in the Red Sea, awnings remained in place twenty-four hours a day.

Deck life meant deck sports. But before any formal deck games were played, someone inevitably convened an amusement committee. Admission was charged for deck sports, a kind of gymkhana at sea; one-and-tuppenny entry fees offset the expense of childrens' prizes. For young passengers, the sports committee organized a full competitive program including wheelbarrow races, sack races, three-legged races, potato races, egg-and-spoon races, skipping contests, and, as finale, a tug of war.

But deck sports were not only for children. Their parents were dragooned into adult races, competition that always divided participants into opposing, male/female sides. Thus segregated, the sexes faced each other in rows at opposite ends of the deck. When the whistle blew for the start of the Cigarette Race, gentlemen ran to their distaff partners with an unlit cigarette in their mouth. Each lady had to light the cigarette—only one match allowed—and the first gentleman back at the starting point puffing away won the race.

Next on tap, keeping the identical teams, might be a Telegram Race. Gentlemen scribbled a ten-word telegram on a slip of paper and then tore down the deck to deliver it to their opposite number. Each lady had to read it and then compose a suitable response as speedily as possible, handing it back to the gentleman who raced home. (Required topics for this two-way telegraphese have not been recorded.)

Yet another popular grown-up competition was the Threadneedle Race. Gentlemen ran down the deck carrying a length of cotton to their lady partners, each of whom held a needle. Once the needle had been successfully threaded, both members of the winning couple had to be first back at the starting post.

On larger vessels with adequate deck space, an obstacle course for gentlemen was set up along the hurricane deck. Among the obstacles was a water jump—created from a tarpaulin rigged to enclose a depth of sea water—as well as open-ended barrels suspended above the deck through which contestants had

Lloyd Triestino

to slither to victory. In the Red Sea, the water jump proved less hazard than halcyon; also-rans tended to linger within it, content to come in last but cooler.

But organized races were special events. Every day, standard deck games included shuffleboard and quoits as well as an eastern shipboard specialty called dumps or bull. Similar to shuffleboard, the game was played with beanbags rather than wooden discs. They were thrown at an inclined board, on which shuffleboard's numbered squares had been painted with special additions. At the two top corners, bracketing highest-scoring ten, were lettered "Bs" or a picture of a bull. Players whose beanbag landed on those corners had ten points deducted from their score. More experienced players tried to hit each number in sequence, counting the two "bull" corners as eleven and twelve. One observer of the period suggested that bull was "a favorite with the young people, on account of the long waits, which afford opportunities for mild flirtation." Another game was called sea quoits or buckets, in which rope rings had to be tossed inside a bucket. After dark, indoor amusements included chess, whist, euchre, cribbage, and backgammon.

Not surprisingly, for the British, the most compelling and popular outdoor sport was deck cricket. It was played with a soft ball, many of which were clouted over the side, though pursers had nets strung to prevent this. It was not, surprisingly, a sport denied distaff passengers. When teams of lady cricketers challenged the gentlemen, the latter would gallantly bowl and bat left-handed to even the odds.

Nearing Malta, the passenger body coalesced, and, as inevitable as seasickness, hard and fast cliques began forming. Like-minded shipmates cherishing the same convictions tended to group together in immutable gatherings, sharing meals, deck chairs, and, always, the same opinions. Betting and gambling proliferated. Passage east passengers bet on everything, from daily mileage totals to what time the vessel would tie up, or, to even more obscure wagering minutia: which foot would the pilot place first on the Jacob's ladder?

The first baggage room day arrived, never an entirely satisfactory occasion. Summoned below on schedule, passengers queued in the alleyway at the top of the lowest companionway until called down by the shirt-sleeved baggage officer and his lascar crew. Because of space limitations in the cabin, the clothing

traffic was two-way: passengers retrieving fresh clothing customarily deposited unwanted clothing in its place. Inevitably, some trunks or dress baskets could not be found. "Then they try and get you to explain how it looks," reported one exasperated matron. "You describe it, then you finally give up, resolved to wear the same clothes for the rest of the voyage."

During the ship's stopover in Valetta on the island of Malta, passengers invariably went ashore, either to buy lace, take refreshment, or see the historic sights. Many purposely lingered ashore to avoid the voyage's first ordeal of coaling. The vessel had steamed 2,290 miles from London and bunkers were nearly empty. Only an hour after the vessel arrived, she was boomed away from the pier. Sailors rigged special staging over the sides and unbolted coal ports along both flanks. Grimy coal barges laden with an army of coal heavers converged on the vessel, tying up alongside the length of the hull. With baskets of coal balanced precariously atop their heads, relays of sweating, blackened figures began their soul-destroying ritual. An endless human chain clambered up teetering gangplanks and tipped their basket-loads down into the bunkers before returning for more.

Within moments, the entire vessel, inside and out, was covered with a choking pall of dust. Though stewards tried covering louvered cabin doors with canvas baffles, the dust inevitably seeped through. For those passengers remaining on board, the torment of coaling involved not only the dust and periodic rattle of anthracite tumbling into bunkers but also the singsong badinage of the coal-heavers, shouting at each other over the noise of their labors. Once coaling was completed and passengers had "tubbed and shampooed," habitual Valetta amusement was that time-honored shipboard perquisite of throwing pennies down to the water to be retrieved by "naked beggars."

As the vessel steams on to Port Said, we should go forward for a glimpse of Second Class, quite often home for officers who had overspent during London leave; by traveling back out to India Second Class, they could save £33. Having previously traveled First Class, they most envied their shipmates aft who were enjoying dinner while they made do with high tea, or, as one ironically described it, "*souper à la fourchette*." In fact, meals in the Second saloon were perfectly edible, and, several times each week, a ship's officer would dine there to ensure that food was as it should be.

Perhaps the best flavor of catering standards in P&O's Second Class may be derived from a scathing report published and circulated by a group of disaffected Indian Army officers—The Passenger and Shipper's Defence League—

Rotterdamsche Lloyd Scheepvaart Maatschappij

who resented not only what they felt to be P&O's monopoly but the company's high prices as well. (P&O was scarcely a monopoly; those disgruntled military men could just as easily have booked on rival British lines or French and German competitors.) This is what they had to say about P&O's shipboard fare:

"High Tea in the Second Class is a deliberate insult to the common sense of Anglo-Indians, who are in constant combat with the dyspeptic incidents of life in the East. You expect them to sit down at the close of the day, under the inaction of boardship life, to slabs of cold meat and greasy imitations of Melton Mowbray pies, with no condiment but bread, director's jams, and dissolving butter, washed down by decoctions of tea. If the repast were designed for robust English navvies, it would be unwholesome even for them. Dairy and meat at the close of an inactive day on a tropical sea are physiological incompatibles and directly invoke a fit of dyspepsia."

But Second Class had some compensation. There was little pretension there and few parvenus. On one vessel returning westbound, a disgruntled First Class passenger reported that the saloon was overrun by "pork-proud purlieus of Chicago and Australian sheep farmers who, having made their pile, had abandoned their shanties for the first time to take in the continong."

One well-satisfied Second Class passenger wrote of his passage east to the *Times* of London. Together with his wife and two children, he had been accommodated forward in a four-berthed cabin on the *Oriental*, equipped with electric light, two portholes, wire mattresses, with everything maintained "as nice and clean as possible." The Saloon he judged spacious, well-lit, airy, with a capacity of fifty people. "We had a separate bar, barman, and pantry, and were allowed to use the portside hurricane deck."

He documented every mouthful. Breakfast was served at 0830, dinner at 1330 (a large midday meal was Second Class's inescapable custom) and High Tea at 1830. For breakfast, "there was porridge, fresh fish, beefsteak or mutton chop, one dish of eggs, another dish of curry, well cooked and plentiful, better than First Class some years ago." Midday dinner consisted of "soup, joint, two entrees or one entree and poultry, pudding, a sweet dish and dessert, any amount of ice—occasionally iced fruits and ice creams made in London." For tea, he

enjoyed "cold fish, sardines, herring or lobster salad, two dishes of cold meats, and jams."

Fellow passengers he found perfectly agreeable. "Two or three missionaries, a doctor or two, two or three army men, some tradesmen, and the servants of some of the First Class passengers. A wife and daughter of a colonel in the artillery, a forest officer, and others whom I could not make out. As we were allowed to use half the hurricane deck, we were able to meet our friends in the first saloon on equal terms."

Sometimes, "servants of the First Class" enjoyed the same accommodations as their masters. On board P&O's *Australia* bound from Melbourne to Colombo, a passenger named Donovan objected strenuously to the purser about one of the men seated at his table. He was the servant of a chronic invalid, and, even though his employer had paid for his servant's First Class fare, Donovan insisted that he be moved either to Second Class or at least to another table. He tried inciting his tablemates to complain without success.

More praise for life in the Second Class came from formerly First Class passengers aboard the *Khedive*. "Our cabin is tiny but you have no idea the difference it makes being forward instead of aft. Last evening, while the First Class were at dinner, we went on to the quarter deck to look round. The vibration from the screws was most unpleasant and we felt glad that our cabin was in so much better a position...The cabins and the ordering of are the same as the first, with everything as sweet and clean. The attendance is very good. There is only one bathroom for ladies and it is not a marble one like the first class baths but one is treated just the same in the matter of salt water and a tin foot tub of fresh."

"The second saloon," the letter continued, "is nicer than the first, and it goes across the ship and has windows open...The food is excellent...See from the menus that they don't stint the food. I should not mind coming Second Class again."

Passengers of all classes were summoned to meals by bugle calls, blown by the cornetist of the steward's band that played out on deck every morning. In fact, there were two bugled summonses each evening, one to dress and another to dine. Amateur musicians among the passenger body performed for their fellows during on-deck evening concerts—another responsibility of the ship's amusement committee—but non-players were specifically enjoined to stay away from the ship's piano. "People who cannot play are very fond of strumming on the piano. At home probably this matters very little to anybody; on board ship, it may annoy hundreds," admonished one piece of company literature. P&O dining saloons boasted another musical instrument, a Chinese gong. With a single reverberating stroke, the head waiter would signal his corps of stewards to remove the soup course and serve the fish.

Before leaving the Mediterranean, it is worth recording some of the terrifying events of Sunday night, April 17, 1887, for passengers aboard P&O's *Tasmania*, bound from Bombay to Marseilles. At 4 A.M., in the midst of a gale, she ran catastrophically aground off Point Roccapina on Corsica's southern coast. Traveling at thirteen knots, *Tasmania* tore her forward bottom plating out, admitting tons of seawater and plunging bow first beneath the waves. The 120 passengers and 161 crew sought refuge in what was left of the vessel's after portion. Four of eight lifeboats had been shattered but the balance were used to ferry passengers across three miles of intervening rough sea to the barren Corsican coast.

Aboard *Tasmania* that night was our indefatigable correspondent Lizzie Bradford. "Well, they sent up rockets—but of course no-one saw them, & then they tried to get out the boats...they took four hours to launch three, they were so stiff and the apparatus so rusty & all this time the sea was dashing furiously over further every minute...Would you believe it, that this was the moment that some of the Stewards took off to loot cabins that were out of the water?...The cold was great and a high cold wind freezing us."

While Lizzie and her children huddled for warmth ashore in a primitive Corsican farmhouse, her husband Edward and dozens of male passengers and crew sought refuge within the ship's smoking room at the stern, the only surviving interior. Eighty people were jammed into a space no more than eighteen feet square, battered by enormous waves throughout the night and following day. Since every window was broken, men took cushions from the settees and braced them with their backs against the force of waves seeking entry. That stifling little smoking room would serve as both shelter and dungeon for twenty-four claustrophobic hours until the steam yacht *Norseman* and the liner *Persévérent* managed to take off the exhausted occupants. A total of thirty-four of *Tasmania*'s people, including Captain Perrin, lost their lives in the wreck. Surviving passengers were taken back to England on board the *Chusan* which had steamed at top speed from Marseilles. Although calm seas were the norm for vessels negotiating passage east or the reverse, spring storms in the Mediterranean could—and did—prove occasionally disastrous.

Starting from Bombay in 1853, a network of steam railways was built across India until it covered the length and breadth of the subcontinent, a total, by the end of the century, of 40,000 miles of track.

Gibraltar from the east.

Port Said lay a thousand miles from Malta. There, since Aden, the next coaling port, was nearly 1,400 miles further away, additional coal was taken aboard. Those passengers who ventured ashore returned after only a brief look around because, then as now, there was really nothing of interest to see. Port Said was a mere sea and rail terminal, as devoid of charm as a frontier crossing. Before the vessel moved into the canal entry, Cairo-bound passengers disembarked for a rail journey to the capital.

Daylight transit south to Suez was a spectators' delight, that part of the passage east that probably aroused the keenest passenger interest. The vessel and its occupants were penetrating the very heart of the Middle East, abandoning Mediterranean waters for those of the Red Sea. For much of the route by daylight, passengers, as they still do today, congregated heavily along the railings—forward vantage points the most hotly contested—until the merciless sun drove them into the shade. In the mid-nineties, the navigable channel averaged seventy-five feet wide so that oncoming vessels passed at extremely close range. Scenery to either side lacked the mountainous jungle variety of Panama, being merely a succession of interminable dunes stretching into the sun-shimmering desert. Occasional camel trains, flocks of vibrantly colored flamingos, or the exciting proximity of passing vessels provided the only visual relief.

By night, passage was cooler. There was electric illumination along the length of the banks as well as on the prow of every vessel. Powerful searchlights were trained ahead of the vessel, vital nocturnal equipment for pilots to spot the succession of buoys delineating channels across Lake Timsah and Bitter Lakes. Along the entire length of the canal, steam dredges hissed and clattered, working around the clock to keep the water's depth in navigational trim.

The port of Suez marked exit from the canal as well as entry into the Red Sea, inaugurating without question the most trying portion of passage east. The distance southeast toward Aden was 1,308 miles. Orient Line vessels, denied the use of P&O's Aden bunkering facilities, coaled on the island of Diego Garcia in the Indian Ocean.

Suez lies exactly on the 30th parallel of latitude north and journeying south mandated entry within one of the hottest sea routes on earth. As degrees of latitude decreased, increments of mercury rose relentlessly. Aboard the outbound steamer *Orient* in the summer of 1887, a graph of noon temperatures was plotted. From a high of ninety-two degrees at Suez, the temperature fell below eighty only twice in the length of the Red Sea.

Of course, from shipboard's air-conditioned present to that punka'd or electric fanned past, it is almost incomprehensible for present-day passengers to share the lament of a P&O diarist from the 1890s: "Scorching, roasting heat never leaves us." Two factors, one climatic and the other socio-sartorial, contributed to his discomfort. First, the Red Sea was ruffled by very few breezes, particularly its northernmost reaches; remember that P&O's sailing colliers could not penetrate as far north as Suez. What wind there was might be a following breeze, wreathing the vessel in a perpetual cloud of its own stack gasses. After several hours of this torture, masters used to reverse course for a few miles to clear the fetid decks and companionways.

Second, one only has to look at on-deck scenes of the period to realize that Victorian clothing standards on even the hottest days never relented. In one of Harry Furniss's classic P&O shipboard sketches, entitled "A Red Sea-iesta," dozing gentlemen sport ties, collars, and jackets while the women, certainly corseted, wore their habitual long skirts and high-necked shirt-waists.

Conversely, at night, sensible deshabille prevailed. Part of the awning rigging left in place for Red Sea passage involved not only horizontal roofs against the sun but also vertical canvas curtains that could be drawn to divide the decks into makeshift, male/female dormitories. On hot nights in the Red Sea, an unvarying evening ritual obtained. Dinner over, passengers might gather on deck for a concert or singsong. Then they would formally bid each other good night and descend, for as little time as possible, to the insufferable heat of their cabins. Their mattresses, sheets, and pillows were gone, already taken up on deck by obliging stewards. Husbands donned their new pajama suits, sensible clothing of Far Eastern origin, from the Hindu pae (leg) jamah (clothing), while their wives changed into traditional nightgown and peignoir.

Then they would ascend to the hurricane deck, each into their own sexually segregated dormitory. Separated husbands and wives would sleep until just after dawn, when lascar crewmen armed with hoses and holystones would rout them out so that the immutable morning scrubdown of every open deck could proceed.

Passage south continued into a veritable cauldron. Initially welcomed at Gibraltar, the sun became the unrelenting enemy. Additional side awnings were rigged to foil its heat in the afternoon. The vessel's hull and superstructure heated

Bombay, the Gateway of India, which was built in 1927 to commemorate the Royal Visit of 1912. It was the scene of the final British departure in 1947.

up day by day and from washroom taps—hot and cold alike—dribbled water the temperature of blood. "I have sweated through a flannel shirt and white jacket," complained one over-dressed passenger. Red Sea temperatures in the boiler room constantly exceeded 120 degrees.

Out on deck, competition lagged. Long, hammocked siestas became the order of every day and the ship's surgeon treated cases of prickly heat and sunburn among the children. The advantage inherent in the enviable company acronym POSH—Port Out, Starboard Home—that ticket agents initialed on favored passengers' tickets, was never more gratifying than during these stifling days; cabins on the shaded side of the vessel were infinitely more bearable than their opposite numbers baking to starboard.

Occasionally, during winters, the Red Sea could be cool and sometimes stormy. Wrote Lizzie Bradford in her diary aboard *Malma* during a February 1874 passage to Bombay: "They terrify us with accounts of bad weather lately in the Red Sea & a tornado in the Gulf of Suez...A strong wind and following sea, & it is very cool and pleasant...Much calmer and they opened the portholes this morning..." But the norm was unrelenting heat and portholes that stayed open for days on end.

After a week of intolerable sea days, the lure of a port—any port— hovered dreamlike beyond the horizon. But one glimpse of long-awaited Aden dispelled any sense of anticipated relief. Romanticized as "the Gibraltar of the East," Aden was a sere, arid spot, dismissed by more than one passenger as "a cinder heap." The port is surrounded by barren cliffs of rock, painted, a passenger water colorist suggested, with a "hellish palette: Brick red, sulfurous yellow and Tartarean black."

P&O had established huge coal reserves here, not entirely for bunkering vessels. Some was used to power a salt water distillation plant to replenish vessels' reserve tanks. With annual rainfall unpredictable, that failsafe was a necessity. Whatever rain did fall was husbanded in Aden's elaborate system of reservoirs, the earliest of which had been laboriously excavated out of bedrock starting in 600 A.D. Passengers who ventured ashore to inspect the reservoirs were warned about the heat: "The climate of Aden is not unhealthy," P&O's guide book assured travelers, "but the heat is great during S.W. monsoons, not only from the sun's rays but also from the radiation produced by the color of the rock."

Those shore excursionists did not tarry long for Aden stopovers were brief, limited to the amount of time it took to coal ship. After more "tubbing and shampooing," passengers and their vessel steamed towards the Indian Ocean. Once around Cape Guardafui, ocean breezes came over the bow, welcome relief from the previous days' sultry passage south. Slowly but surely, the even tenor of normal shipboard life resumed, the most trying part of the voyage now past.

P. Henderson & Co.

It was not only the most trying but the most pungent as well: prelude from Tilbury to Aden served, to my mind, as the archetypal passage east. Once past Aden, horizons broadened. Divergent ocean tracks spread out in a fan as passage east continued to the far side of the globe, to Bombay, Colombo, Madras, Calcutta, Melbourne, Singapore, Hong Kong, or Yokohama. Some would disembark at Colombo to board steamers that would carry them further east. Destinations printed on luggage tags and mail sacks would be achieved after further weeks of conventional ocean travel.

But it was passage east's preliminary, sandy bottleneck that had set the shipboard tone. All tonnage destined for the East endured that obligatory confinement before resumption of normal sea days. The Egyptian interlude involved first encounter with the exotic as well as overland interruption or canal transit before the Red Sea's equatorial approach.

Sailing transatlantic westbound, passage to America ended abruptly; after a week's featureless crossing, the voyage was suddenly over at Ambrose light ship, prelude to the spires of Manhattan. But passage east was a far more complex and picturesque immersion, a cumulative unveiling of locale and climate. Each way station imparted its own distinctive flavor to the Eastern blend. Coincidentally, those flotillas of vessels and their itineraries established the maritime groundwork for much of the present-day cruise industry.

Once at their destination and nostalgically inclined, most—but not all— passengers regretted leaving their vessel. Last word from Lizzie Bradford, written from Bombay's Elphinstone Hotel in 1866: "Here we are once more on dry land and I need not say very delighted to have done now altogether with that horrid ship and sea." Her disaffection may well have been triggered by Bombay's traditionally chaotic disembarkations which always took place at night. Luggage inevitably went astray or was picked up by the wrong party.

We have, suiting the nature of our mandate, persevered east. The mood on board vessels making the return passage was far more subdued, doubtless because the proportion of invalids was high. P&O archives are filled with reports of passengers in extremis embarking to return home. A captain of the Argyle and Sutherland Highlanders, carried aboard at Singapore in a state of near death, credited his full recovery without question to the ministrations of his steward LeMarne who "looked after me selflessly."

Royal Navy Deputy Inspector General Belgrave Ninnis was ill with dysentery, traveling from Hong Kong as far as Colombo on the *Thames* before transferring to *Coromandel* for passage to England; he wrote to thank both chief stewards and ships' surgeons for aiding his recuperation. Aboard the *Valetta* under command of Captain Briscoe—commended by many past passengers—Rhoda Watson traveled with a sick sister; she wrote to thank the commander for the "almost parental care extended to me while his goodness to my sick sister has commanded the admiration of everyone on board."

A high cast Brahmin traveling on the *Peking* with two of his own Hindu servants penned an effusive letter of thanks to the surgeon for resuscitating his "very sick friend on board, an S.N. Ahamed, for whom very little hope had been contemplated;" he was, according to the grateful writer, "restored to life." A New Zealand bishop informed the head office that he was crippled and had to be carried on deck, but thanks to Purser Bentley and his steward, John Herbert, survived the passage to England admirably.

Indirect comment on the long sick lists aboard homebound tonnage can be derived from the remark made by a stewardess to Miss Roper, who, concluding a solo circumnavigation of the globe, had boarded *Oceana* at Gibraltar. Her dedicated paragon of a company servant refused a proffered tip: "Really, madam, I have been of so little service to you through having to attend to the cases of illness that I cannot take anything from you."

And, finale to this glimpse of the English abroad, a glimpse of their return, exchanging India's heat and dust for England's gentle countryside. Helen Ford, just arrived back on the *Peninsular*, concludes with a touching paean to home: "A soft, sweet day and the auriculas and daffodils are out. I hear the cuckoo. Here ends my Indian diary."

On Board Bibliography

Cable, Boyd. *The Hundred Year History of the P&O.* London: Ivor Nicholson and Watson, 1937.

Furniss, Harry. *P&O Sketches in Pen and Ink.* London: George Weidenfeld & Nicolson Ltd, 1987.

Howarth, David and Stephen. *The Story of P&O.* London: Weidenfeld and Nicolson, 1986.

Lloyd, W.W. *P&O Pencillings.* London: Day & Son, n.d.

Maber, John M. *North Star to Southern Cross.* Prescot: T. Stephenson & Sons Ltd., 1967.

MacDonald, Bryan Ed. *Dearest Mother, The Letters of F.R. Kendall.* London: Lloyds of London Press, Ltd, 1988.

McCullough, David. *The Path Between the Seas.* New York: Simon & Schuster, 1977.

Mencken, August. *First-Class Passenger.* New York: Alfred A. Knopf, 1938.

Morris, Charles F. *Origins, Orient and Oriana.* Brighton: Teredo Books Ltd, 1980.

Padfield, Peter. *Beneath the House Flag of the P&O.* London: Hutchinson, 1981.

Rabson, Stephen & Kevin O'Donoghue. *P&O A Fleet History.* Kendal: World Ship Society, 1988.

An Argyll motorcar which, like so many of the ships, was also built on the Clyde, c. 1910.

Singapore, Keppel Harbour.

Shipping in the Hooghly with Howrah Bridge, 1880s.

Shipping in the Hooghly, Calcutta, 1890s.

Calcutta. Shipping in the Hooghly, 1937.

*The departure of H.M. King George V and Queen Mary from
Bombay, January 12, 1912.*

Singapore, Raffles Hotel, 1897.

Plate 27.

Discharging and Loading, Singapore, 1910

The great majority of shipping on world trade routes consisted of tramp steamers. These were cargo ships which did not follow a regular timetable but went from one port to another to pick up cargoes as instructed by their managers. Their choice of ports of call depended on fluctuations in trade.

From the Cape of Good Hope, the shortest route to the China Sea lies via the Straits of Sunda and the island of Java, but when the Suez Canal was opened, ships from Europe would rather steam more directly by the Straits of Malacca. Singapore rose to importance as an entrepôt as well as a port serving its own hinterland.

It is appropriate to illustrate, therefore, the traffic that came and went by tramp steamer in a painting of the roadstead at Singapore. As in most ports outside Europe, there were no deepwater berths; cargo ships had to discharge and load from lighters brought alongside.

Ships in this view include a typical three island cargo steamer belonging to the Clan Line, a passenger cargo liner of Messageries Maritimes bound for Saigon, and a tramp with the markings of Thos. and Jno. Brocklebank. Local products which are likely to figure on the manifests include Malayan rubber and tin.

Plate 28.

HMS *Medina* at Prinsep's Ghat, Calcutta, 1912

Only once during the whole period of British rule in India did the reigning monarch visit the Subcontinent. This was in 1911, when King George V and Queen Mary sailed from England on board a brand new P & O liner, *Medina*, which was chartered from the company and commissioned into the Royal Navy for the voyage.

The King-Emperor landed with pomp and circumstance at Bombay, entering the country under a temporarily erected "Gateway of India" on the Apollo Bunder. The principal event of the Royal visit was the Great Durbar at Delhi, a glittering ceremony where it was announced that the seat of government was to be moved from Calcutta to the ancient Mogul Emperors' capital at Delhi.

The Royal party traveled from Bombay to Calcutta on board HMS *Medina*, and they came ashore at Prinsep's Ghat. (The King, as a Naval Officer, would have been a stickler for having his ship turned in naval fashion to head towards the open sea before he disembarked.)

Prinsep's Ghat is a charming stone pavilion composed of Ionic columns, built to provide shelter at the landing stage and to commemorate the life of James Prinsep, antiquary, linguist, and Master of the Mint. He was the first to translate the rock edicts of Asoka, and he was responsible for introducing a uniform coinage and system of weights and measures throughout the country in the early nineteenth century.

The King and Queen disembarked onto flats moored between ship and shore which were shaded with awnings. The guard of honor may well have been mounted by a Scottish Highland regiment, and the splendid lancers of the Viceroy's Bodyguard would have been in evidence to escort the Viceregal carriage to Government House.

One of the less important events attended by their Majesties was the Calcutta Turf Club horse show at the Tollygunge Club. Second Prize in the Pony Jumping Competition was won by George Marshall on Convent Girl. The trophy, a silver rose bowl, was presented to my father by Queen Mary.

After her return to England, *Medina* was deprived of her third mast (which had been borrowed from another ship building for P & O at Caird's yard to enable her to wear the proper show of flags for a Royal Yacht), and her white paint was obliterated with the standard P & O black and tan. Then she entered service for the first time as a passenger liner.

Plate 29.

SS *Mongara*, Gibraltar, 1914

The extraordinarily graceful British India Line steamer *Mongara* sweeps away from the Rock of Gibraltar early one morning in April 1914. She was on her maiden voyage to Calcutta. The vessel's gross registered tonnage was 8,200, and her triple-expansion engines drove two shafts and screws giving her a service speed of 13 knots.

The British India line, or BI as it was generally known, was already the world's largest shipping line when it merged, later that year, with the more famous P & O. Founded in 1856, its operations were centered on the Indian Ocean.

Two Scottish merchants, William Mackinnon and Robert Mackenzie, started the company in Calcutta with ships sailing from there to ports in Burma. By 1862 operations were extended to a coastwise service from Calcutta all the way around India and Ceylon to Karachi, calling at two dozen ports along the way.

Throughout its existence, BI was closely allied with shipping agencies and trading companies such as MacKinnon, Mackenzie & Co., Smith Mackenzie, Binny's, and Gellately, Hankey, Sewell & Co.

The shipping line steadily extended the scope of its operations in step with the inexorable growth of world trade during the second half of the nineteenth century. Its vessels were sent throughout the Persian Gulf, they plied to Aden, and from there, regular services were introduced to ports all down the east coast of Africa, to Mombasa, Zanzibar, and Madagascar. From Rangoon the system was extended to the Straits Settlements, Penang, Malacca, and Singapore, and subsequently to Java and other parts of the Dutch East Indies. Subsidiary companies were established there and in Queensland, Australia. Eventually BI introduced scheduled services all the way back to Britain, and its eastern network was enlarged as far as Hong Kong, Shanghai, Japan, New Zealand, Mauritius, and Durban. A related company named Macneill & Co. operated fleets of river steamers on the Irrawaddy and the Ganges river systems.

Almost all the leading figures in the business were Scots, as were a large proportion of those who inaugurated the great trading companies of the East and the banks which followed them. *Mongara* was Tyne-built, but most BI ships, unsurprisingly, were built on the Clyde, although many of them spent all their working lives far from home waters. By the time the last one was withdrawn from scheduled service in 1982, the company had owned and operated a total of 532 ships.

Gibraltar, looking towards Morocco, c. 1860.

Plate 30.

RMS *Kaisar-i-Hind*, Port Said, 1914

Located at the northern entrance to the Suez Canal, Port Said was an artificial port constructed where the dredged channel through coastal lakes and marshlands reached the open sea. A mole was built on the western side 1 3/4 miles long out into the Mediterranean, midway along which was erected a giant statue of Ferdinand de Lesseps in tribute to the creator of the Canal. Ships had to moor in mid-channel while awaiting their turn in a southbound convoy. Transit of the 87-mile long canal took 15 hours, and in 1913, as many as 6,000 vessels passed through the waterway.

The P & O liner *Kaisar-i-Hind* was completed shortly before the outbreak of war in 1914. The largest built for the company to that date, she had a measurement of 11,400 tons gross, quadruple-expansion engines with twin screws providing a top speed of 18.5 knots, and she carried 550 passengers. On her maiden voyage to Bombay she made a record time of just under 18 days from Tilbury.

The passenger list is unlikely to have included many tourists. Four generations of British in India were brought up to regard the ebb and flow of passage on stately ships of P & O as a familiar and inevitable part of the pattern of life.

Behind the ship can be seen the distinctive Port Said Lighthouse tower, silhouetted against a sunset sky inflamed by dust over the Western Desert.

Shanghai, the Bund, 1923. The Hong Kong-Shanghai Bank.

Plate 31.

SS *Johan de Witt* Lying off the Bund, Shanghai, 1921

The Stoomboot Maatschappij "Nederland," or Netherlands Steamship Line, operated primarily between the Netherlands and the Far East via Algiers, Genoa, Port Said, Suez, Colombo, and Singapore. The terminus was Batavia, now Jakarta, capital of the great archipelago that comprised the Netherlands East Indies. Other services were operated to China, Japan, the Philippines, Australia, and American Pacific coast ports.

The second great Dutch shipping line to the East was the Rotterdam Lloyd; between them they set up, in 1881, the K.P.M., or Royal Packet Line, to take over the local routes operated up till then by a Java-based subsidiary of the British India Line.

Johan de Witt was a 10,500-ton liner built in Rotterdam for the Netherlands Line in 1920. She was a twin-screw turbine vessel capable of 16 knots.

Shanghai in the 1920s was one of the world's major trading ports, the focus of enormous foreign investment in China, and it was the scene of massive construction.

The *Johan de Witt* discharging cargo in midstream is pictured from the Bund, the famous street on top of the embankment that contains the river. The principal commercial buildings were constructed along this riverfront, ponderous steel-framed and stone-faced palaces in classical-revival style, counterparts of those that line the Thames Embankment in London. They included the premises of the great Eastern trading houses such as Jardine Mathesons, the Customs House, the Mercantile Bank of India, and the Hong Kong-Shanghai Bank.

SS Amra, *surrounded by lighters at Rangoon, 1938.*

Plate 32.

SS *Leconte de Lisle*, Haiphong, 1924

Passengers have congregated along the rails to watch those who are disembarking into launches to take them ashore in the steamy tropical heat at Haiphong, French Indo-China. The house flag of Messageries Maritimes at the mainmast, two black Ms on a white ground defined with red corners, signifies the premier French shipping line in the Eastern trade.

Note the canvas awnings spread to provide shade on deck, pierced with holes for the masts and derricks. There is a profusion of white ventilators which supply the cabins in addition to the big, black boiler room air intakes; air conditioning was not available in those days.

Plate 33.

SS *Mulbera*, Grand Harbour, Malta, 1924

It used to be the custom for Maltese women, when they went outside the house, to wear *faldettas*, black shrouded garments that envelop the wearer and which look much like the hood of a carriage. Some ladies can be seen here descending a narrow alley in the limestone fortress city of Valetta. At the foot of the street lies a sun-splashed quay and dancing waters across which ply the Maltese *dghaisas*. These craft with their high prows and sterns, sometimes equipped with white cotton canopies, are propelled by standing and pushing the oars forward rather than by pulling or, like gondolas, by a single sweep.

Fort St. Angelo, the stronghold of La Valette, Grand Master of the Knights of St. John during the Great Siege, lies across the harbor, but it is largely obscured in this view by the temporary presence of the British India Line steamer *Mulbera*.

Mulbera was launched by Alexander Stephen & Sons of Linthouse, Glasgow, in 1922. She was 9,100 tons gross, had steam turbines geared to twin screws, and carried 170 passengers in a single class.

Typical of many passenger-cargo vessels that operated through the Suez Canal, *Mulbera* was one of eight sister ships belonging to the British India line. On this voyage, in December 1924, she was carrying the Duke and Duchess of York to Mombasa on a visit to Kenya. The royal couple passed through the Canal on another occasion, in June 1927, on their return journey from Australia in the battle cruiser HMS *Renown*. The Duchess is now known as the greatly admired and respected Queen Elizabeth the Queen Mother.

Plate 34.

RMS *Orama*, Naples, 1926

The Orient Line placed orders with Vickers-Armstrongs of Barrow-in-Furness for five 20,000-ton turbine-engined passenger liners which were completed between 1924 and 1929. They were designed to operate the mail and passenger service between London and Australia, and as with all the company's ships, their names began with O. The *Orama*'s sister ships were called *Orford, Oronsay, Orontes,* and *Otranto.* Each carried over a thousand passengers, of which two-thirds were in Third Class, intended for immigrants.

During the course of the First World War, steam turbines proved themselves conclusively to be more efficient as well as more reliable than reciprocating machinery, and in warships, the introduction of oil fuel showed tremendous advantages over coal as the means of raising steam. In the immediate postwar years, therefore, many existing merchant ships had their boilers converted to use oil, and all new steamships built thereafter incorporated turbine propulsion as well as oil-fired boilers.

Orient Line ships in those days had black hulls with white upperworks, red boot topping, buff funnels and ventilators, and black funnel caps similar to those found on warships of the Royal Navy. Characteristically, their passenger liners had two or more open verandah decks around the stern, covered but not enclosed by glass. This feature provided more light and fresh air to cabins on the lower decks, but it would have been impracticable for ships which had to ride the heavy seas of winter in the North Atlantic.

Gross tonnage is a measurement of enclosed volume, not weight, and therefore, ships the same size as *Orama* might well have substantially higher tonnage, giving a misleading impression of relative size.

Bought by its great rival the P & O company in 1918, the Orient Line continued to operate separately for 40 years, but it scheduled different ports of call along the route. These included Toulon, Palma, and Naples. *Orama* is portrayed under a threatening sky in Naples roads in 1926.

In the background Mount Vesuvius is exhausting just a very faint wisp of smoke from the crater. Fishing craft are scuttling for safe harbor.

Plate 35.

RMS *Viceroy of India* Leaving Tilbury, 1929

Government clerks, known as *babus*, were notorious in India for their pedantic dedication to paperwork. Confronted by the creaking apparatus of this massive bureaucracy, Lord Curzon, the grandest of Viceroys, is credited by Jan Morris with this exasperated observation: "Like the diurnal revolution of the earth, went the files, steady, solemn, sure and slow."

The Peninsular and Oriental never went for speed, and the company placed little store in showmanship. It was not until 1928 that it launched its first ship with a splash of grandeur.

In the high-flying spirit of the Twenties, the *Viceroy of India,* designed for the Tilbury-Bombay service, was given more elaborate accommodation than had been seen outside the North Atlantic. Publicity was given to the indoor swimming pool and to the First Class Smoking Room in "Scots Baronial Style," designed by the Hon. Elsie Mackay, daughter of Lord Inchcape, the Chairman of P & O. The ship had cabins for 670 passengers, 415 of which were in First Class.

The ship was interesting technically for the adoption of electric final drive, power originating from conventional steam turbines. This form of propulsion had been pioneered by the U.S. Navy for battleships built in 1917. The *Viceroy* had a measurement of 20,000 tons gross and a service speed of 19 knots. She was built by Alexander Stephen & Sons in Glasgow.

The Thames was lined with industry and crowded with shipping when the *Viceroy of India* made her maiden voyage from Tilbury in 1929, including the well-known Thames spritsail barges carrying coal, gravel, and other short-haul cargoes up and down the Estuary.

A ship commanded by an officer of the Royal Naval Reserve was entitled to wear the Blue Ensign in place of the Red Ensign worn generally by British merchant ships. At the mainmast, the *Viceroy* is flying the P & O Company house flag, which proudly carries the blue and white of the House of Braganza together with the red and yellow of the Bourbons, a privilege which was granted in the company's early years in recognition of services to the royal houses of both Portugal and Spain.

I. H. M.

Zanzibar, the waterfront in the 1880s. The scene today is little different.

Plate 36.

SS *City of Tokio* Entering Kilindini Harbour, Mombasa, 1931

Ellerman Lines ships operated out of Glasgow and Liverpool to the Red Sea, India, and East Africa. The 7,000-ton *City of Tokio*, built at Stockton-on-Tees in 1921, was typical of many smaller vessels in the Hall Line fleet which formed part of the shipping group controlled by Sir John Ellerman. She had geared turbines and a single screw which drove her at 12 knots.

The gray-hulled cargo liner is seen sliding past the ramp of the ferry at Likoni, on her way into Kilindini. At this point, oceangoing ships pass through a surprisingly narrow passage between the island and the mainland to the south; it is an exciting place from which to watch.

British merchantmen were required to carry the Plimsoll Mark. This is a diagram painted on the hull amidships to indicate the minimum safe freeboard. The required freeboard varied according to freshwater or seawater, summer or winter, and tropical or other conditions. The greatest freeboard, and therefore the lightest permitted load of cargo, was that required for operation in "Winter, North Atlantic."

Plate 37.

Embarkation at Tilbury, 1937

If you never ventured ashore at intermediate ports, you would have little opportunity to see the outside of your own ship. On approaching the docks it was hard to catch even a glimpse of topmasts above the cargo sheds, and after that you were completely immersed in the business of shepherding luggage from the train into the hands of the shipping line, keeping count of hand baggage, passport and tickets, and thereafter preoccupied with all the excitement of boarding, finding the way first to the purser's office and finally to your cabin. The end of the journey was likely to be even busier, what with immigration, searching for luggage, running the gauntlet of customs, meeting new colleagues, and all the distractions of coping with uncomprehending natives, unfamiliar currency, and hot, sticky climate.

The view that everyone obtained was something like this one, a dark canyon between cargo shed and the side of the ship, cluttered with sloping gangways and overshadowed by cranes. There would be an accompaniment of groans from the cranes, whine from winches, the clatter of goods wagons, and the panting of a locomotive somewhere out of sight. The general fuss would be punctuated by short, sharp blasts from a tug's steam hooter and the plaintive shriek of gulls.

A painting also cannot convey two further sensations. On going aboard one immediately noticed the smell, a mingling of fuel oil, fresh paint, disinfectant, and other, unidentifiable components. There was, in addition, the experience of motion. At the dockside, this might amount to little more than a faint trembling set up by distant machinery, but the surface underfoot was no longer solid floor but deck. A ship's deck is never an entirely horizontal plane, nor, as long as the ship is afloat, are her decks completely inert.

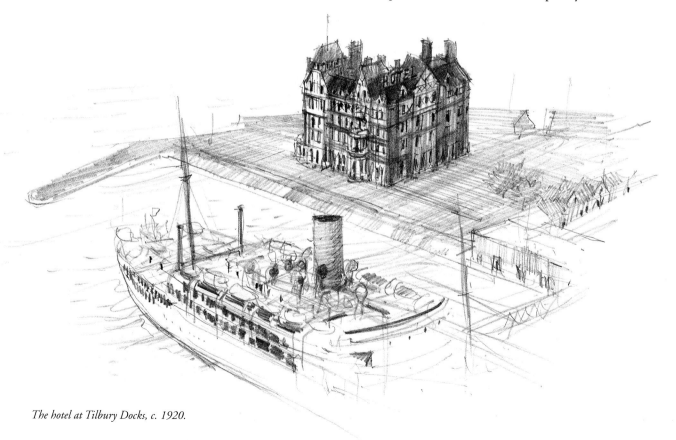

The hotel at Tilbury Docks, c. 1920.

Plate 38.

SS *Mashobra*, Dar es Salaam, 1939

The harbor called Dar es Salaam (Haven of Peace) is enchanting. Situated on the mainland of East Africa, roughly opposite the island of Zanzibar, it comprises a lagoon reached from the open sea through a narrow mouth between low coral headlands. Limpid, blue-green waters are contained within a wide sweep of white sand. The beach is bounded by a grass-covered embankment which is shaded by splendid great mango trees, scarlet flamboyants, and coconut palms. The town of Dar es Salaam has been laid out around this lovely harbor, so the spire of the Lutheran Church rises over the waterfront and black and white verandahs of the dignified old German public buildings can be glimpsed between the trees. The humidity of the tropical coast seems to be constantly tempered by a steady sea breeze which rattles the palm fronds.

Tattered lateen sails belonging to Arabian trading *dhows* and to the outrigger dugout canoes used by local fishermen go scudding to and fro among the shipping in the harbor.

I saw the place first from the deck of the Lloyd Triestino liner *Africa*. Offshore, a tug was secured alongside to provide our ship with additional maneuvering power, and we entered the channel at a fast clip to ensure quick response to the helm. Immediately past the narrows, the pilot rang for "full astern" to arrest the vessel before she ran aground.

The harbor was crowded, and we picked up moorings close to adjoining ships. They seemed to be impossibly close to the gently shelving beach.

Once safely secured fore and aft, green canvas awnings were rigged, and a leisurely lunch was served on deck. We went ashore by launch, for in those days there were only a handful of deepwater berths where a merchantman could be brought alongside for loading.

The ship in the painting is the British India Line steamer *Mashobra*, 8,300 tons gross registered tonnage, which was built by Barclay, Curle & Co of Whiteinch on Clydeside in 1920. She was designed for the London-Calcutta service, but like all BI ships, she had to be prepared to switch routes as the necessity arose.

In 1939 there were over 100 ships in the company's service, 51 of which were to be sunk during the course of the Second World War. *Mashobra* and her sister ship *Manela* were both employed as depot ships for maritime aircraft; they were based in the Orkney islands, the Shetlands, and in Iceland. *Mashobra* was bombed during the Narvik campaign in 1940 and had to be beached and subsequently destroyed. Her sister ship served throughout the war, finally taking part in preparations for the invasion of the Straits of Malacca in 1945. The operation was overtaken by the Japanese surrender, and the *Manela* was discharged from service in 1946.

Plate 39.

RMS *Strathnaver* Leaving Sydney Harbour, 1940

Militarily, the Overland Route was first used during the Crimean War, when troops stationed in India were sent that way to the Black Sea, and once the Suez Canal was open it was regularly used for sending troops to and from India. Regiments from India were shipped via the Canal to Malta in 1885 as a precaution—and a demonstration—during the crisis which very nearly led to war with Russia.

The great strategic importance of the Canal became evident in two world wars. In the first, Empire troops and war materials were sent this way to France and to the landings at Gallipoli, and in the second, to take part in the fighting in North Africa. On a single day in September 1914, 30,000 troops from India arrived at Marseilles in a convoy of 24 ships. British possession of the Canal doomed isolated German forces in East Africa in one war and Italians likewise in the second. On the other hand, the Canal in enemy hands would not only have given them access to oil from the Persian Gulf but also endangered the British position in the entire Indian Ocean region.

This painting is of the big P & O liner *Strathnaver*, the first of five sister ships built in the 1930s for the Australian service and named for Scottish straths, or river valleys. Here she is seen from Sydney Harbour Bridge in wartime guise, crammed with khaki-clad Australian troops bound for Egypt. A light cruiser of the *Leander* class can be seen in the background; she will form part of the convoy escort.

Circular Quay, Sydney, 1890s.

Plate 40.

SS *Strathnaver,* Sydney, 1949

Strathnaver and *Strathaird*, the first of five white liners built for P & O in 1931-1938, had three funnels, two of which were dummies, but the *Strathmore, Stratheden,* and *Strathallan* had only one. During wartime service, the nonfunctional funnels were removed in order to improve the field of fire for antiaircraft guns. Thus when the four surviving ships re-entered the Australian service after the war, they all looked much alike. Compare this 1949 view with the painting of the same ship leaving Sydney with troops on board in 1940. The viewpoint of the first picture is the famous Sydney Harbour Bridge, completed in 1932, which can be seen in the background of this painting.

The liner has just pulled out of Circular Quay and is churning the water as she completes her swing and starts to gain forward motion before heading down Port Jackson towards the open sea. It looks as though she may escape the heavy downpour which is threatening the city of Sydney.

Strathnaver and *Strathaird* were equipped with turbo-electric propulsion, in the same way as the *Viceroy of India,* but the three later ships had normal single-reduction geared steam turbines. The earlier ships were slightly faster at 22 knots. All five ships were built by Vickers-Armstrongs; all had oil-fired boilers and twin screws. Gross tonnage varied between 22,550 and 23,720, and they each carried more than 1,000 passengers.

Mail contracts were not renewed after the Second World War, so the prefix RMS ceased to be applied.

Plate 41.

SS *Uganda*, Mombasa, 1953

The 14,400-ton British India liner *Uganda*, making her way gingerly up the Port of Kilindini, is being met by attentive and immaculate white tugs of the East African Railways and Harbours Administration. She had recently been completed by Barclay, Curle & Co. of Glasgow.

Mombasa Island lies to the right of the picture. On the near (southern) side is the modern port, lined with deepwater berths and rail-served industry. On the far side of the island, facing the mainland to the north, lies the Arab town with its ancient trading links to the Persian Gulf. The old *dhow* harbor there is dominated by Fort Jesus, established by the Portuguese in 1593.

The Island is separated from the mainland to north and south by narrow creeks, the old harbor and Port Tudor to the north, modern Kilindini leading into Port Reitz to the south. Road and railroad leading to upcountry Kenya, and

thence to Uganda, pass across a causeway separating these two bodies of water before starting on the long climb inland.

In 1953 none of the 300 miles of road from Nairobi was paved, except for a heavenly stretch of wartime construction near Mackinnon Road, if I remember. Driving down from the Highlands by night for coolth, we lost count of the sudden stony streambeds which had such destructive effect on tires and shock absorbers, and in the blinding dust there was always a big chance of colliding with game. When we reached the Coast, the humid, languid atmosphere was a blessing, and the tropical vegetation seemed extravagantly lush.

We took the little passenger ferry across the harbor to Mtongwe, passing close by the sparkling black and white cliffside of the *Uganda* which had just put in from Durban. She belonged to another world.

Plate 42.

SS *Orcades* Leaving Table Bay, Cape Town, 1957

In 1935 the Orient Line painted the hull of their new liner *Orion* a beautiful tawny-yellow, officially described as "corn" colored. Thereafter, all new ships adopted the same livery, which was phased out after the fleet was merged with that of the parent company P & O in 1960.

Orcades was the first of three 28,000-ton liners built for Orient in the years 1947-1953 by Vickers-Armstrongs. The others were *Oronsay* and *Orsova.* They were driven by steam turbines with twin screws and had a speed of 22 knots. Each had accommodation for about 1,500 passengers in tourist class plus some 350,000 cu.ft. of cargo capacity, half of it refrigerated.

The Suez Canal was blocked by the Egyptians in November 1956 as a result of the Anglo-French attempt to take possession following nationalization of the Suez Company by President Nasser. Shipping had to be rerouted around Africa, including ships such as *Orcades* on her way from Australia to England; hence her visit to Cape Town depicted in the painting.

On this occasion the canal was cleared within six months by international action. The second closing of the canal in June 1967 lasted for eight years. This had a permanent effect on the pattern of worldwide shipping trade.

Cape Town nestles at the foot of Table Mountain, a 4,000-ft. high rock face more than a mile long which looks north across Table Bay. The mountain is flanked by Devil's Peak to the east and Lion's Head to the west, and southward it extends in a descending ridgeline for some thirty miles terminating in a narrow rocky promontory named the Cape of Good Hope.

Orcades has left Cape Town docks, just visible off her bow, and is setting course northward towards the equator. The *John X. Merriman,* a big oceangoing tug of the South African Railways and Harbours, has just cast off.

The mountain is covered by the famous "table cloth." In the prevailing summer wind, the southeaster, cloud accumulates along the top and continually pours over the northern and western edges, dissipating as it descends.

Cochin, on the Malabar Coast of India, the entrance to the local canal.

Plate 43.

MV *Dwarka,* Cochin, 1958

The 4,850-ton British India passenger-cargo liner *Dwarka* was launched by Swan, Hunter, and Wigham Richardson at Wallsend-on-Tyne in 1946. She was designed for operation between India, the Persian Gulf, and the Red Sea, and in her 35 years of service, she no doubt carried tens of thousands of pilgrims undertaking the *Haj.*

Dwarka is the only ship illustrated in this book which was not powered by steam. As with a steadily increasing proportion of new ships she was a Motor Vessel, equipped with an oil-burning diesel engine, which in her case, had five cylinders and a single screw giving a service speed of 13.5 knots.

Her total passenger accommodation was 1,100, but of this number only 50 traveled in First and Second Class and they alone had cabins. The rest were described as "Berthed Deck" and "Unberthed Deck Passengers."

Cochin is on the Malabar Coast, some 700 miles south of Bombay. It was an important entrepôt during centuries of Arab monopoly over the Indian Ocean trade routes. The Portuguese finally succeeded in penetrating the system in the sixteenth century, and thereafter the most important trading ports were those set up by them, followed successively by Dutch, French, and then English merchants.

In the 1920s the government of British India made a bold attempt to stimulate the economy of the region by creating an up-to-date deepwater port at Cochin. *Dwarka* is here seen negotiating its approaches in 1958, shepherded by the steam tug *Lord Willingdon* and surrounded by native fishing craft. Some might read significance in the presence of a traditional Arab trading *dhow,* still operating commercially in these familiar waters.

Dwarka was the last British India line ship to remain in scheduled passenger service. She was withdrawn and sold for breaking-up in May 1982.

Sydney in 1870.

Plate 44.

SS *Oriana*, Circular Quay, Sydney, 1968

Orient Lines' *Oriana* and her P & O counterpart *Canberra* were the last liners built for the Australian run. Completed in 1960, *Oriana* already had something of the appearance of the great cruise ships which are today the subject of a major passenger-ship revival. More than half her 26-year career was spent exclusively on cruising.

Characteristic of modern cruise ships, *Oriana*'s superstructure seems to pile up dangerously high above the hull. Every device of hull form and weight distribution is employed to maximize the number of decks above waterline and the spaciousness of passenger accommodation with broad windows looking out upon the sea.

Oriana was a ship of 42,000 tons, 800 feet long, and she had cabins for 2,130 passengers. For their last—and by far their largest—ship, the Orient Line remained faithful to Vickers-Armstrongs at Barrow, their favorite shipbuilder. With a designed speed of 27.5 knots, *Oriana* proved capable of maintaining nearly 30 knots in service. This enabled her to make the passage from Tilbury to Sydney in three weeks, which compares with five weeks taken by the first Orient liner in 1883 sailing from London to Adelaide via the Cape.

Long-standing rivalry between the two companies' ships came to an end when the Orient Line was absorbed into P & O in 1960. For five years after her maiden voyage *Oriana* retained the distinctive Orient Line corn-colored hull, but in 1965, she adopted the white livery of P & O. The badge on her stem was never obliterated, but the P & O house flag can be seen flying from the jackstaff in this view.

The oldest and foremost passenger landing place in Sydney, Circular Quay lies in the center of the city and immediately below the universally recognized landmark of Sydney Harbour Bridge.

Plate 45.

SS *Chusan,* Bombay, 1970

The last sailing day from India was February 8, 1970. On that date the P & O liner *Chusan* departed from Ballard Pier, Bombay, the last scheduled passenger liner to do so. She was on her way eastbound, from Britain to Australia and Hong Kong.

This painting portrays the familiar dockside scene: ship's side stitched with rows of portholes, passengers surging up gangways, privileged promenade decks topped by a rank of bulbous lifeboats, and above all, the great yellow stack and bunting fluttering against the sky.

Thus ended an era that had begun in 1837 with the start of the first scheduled service from Bombay to Suez, operated by the East India Company's paddle steamers *Berenice* and *Atalanta*. Ironically, *Chusan* was obliged to make her way home via the Cape, for the Suez Canal was closed from June 1967 to 1975 as a result of the Israeli-Egyptian War.

Chusan had a gross tonnage of 24,000; she could carry a thousand passengers and 430,000 cu.ft. of cargo. Her steam turbines propelled her at 23 knots. After a service career of 23 years she was sold for breaking-up in 1973.

The Royal Bombay Yacht Club, c. 1880.

INDEX